# Traces of Treasure

## Quest for God
## in the Commonplace

# Joanne Lehman

# Traces of Treasure

### Quest for God
### in the Commonplace

HERALD PRESS
Scottdale, Pennsylvania
Waterloo, Ontario

Library of Congress Cataloging-in-Publication Data
Lehman, Joanne, 1950-
        Traces of treasure : quests for God in the commonplace /
Joanne Lehman.
          p.   cm.
        ISBN 0-8361-3655-1
        1. Spiritual life—Mennonite authors. 2. Lehman, Joanne,
1950-    . I. Title.
BV4501.2.L434   1994
248.4'897—dc20

                                                                93-36493
                                                                     CIP

The paper used in this publication is recycled and meets the minimum requirements of American National Standard for Information Sciences—Permanence of Paper for Printed Library Materials, ANSI Z39.48-1984.

TRACES OF TREASURE
Copyright © 1994 by Herald Press, Scottdale, Pa. 15683
        Published simultaneously in Canada by Herald Press,
        Waterloo, Ont. N2L 6H7. All rights reserved
Library of Congress Catalog Number: 93-36493
International Standard Book Number: 0-8361-3655-1
Printed in the United States of America
Book and cover design by Paula Johnson

03 02 01 00 99 98 97 96 95 94 10 9 8 7 6 5 4 3 2 1

*To Ralph,*
*whose love I treasure*

# *Contents*

## Walking in Holiness

# *Foreword*

A FEW YEARS AGO, early one evening with Joanne, I walked around the half section near the Lehman home in Ohio. We talked about writing, about spirituality, about life in general. It became clear to me then that Joanne had little loyalty to a piety that could be dispensed with for the day after fifteen minutes of devotional reading and a short prayer. That was too much like a quick fix—the fast cup of coffee gulped before one hits the day running. And Joanne does a lot of running.

As we walked, she tried to put into words for me her thinking about Christian spirituality. It had to be grounded in contemplation and encompass all of life. To her the devotional life was not a separate segment of life, but "a collection of conscious and subconscious living, which welds thought and action." God-directed thoughts keep meshing with daily activities as mundane as making pancakes for breakfast or as ethereal as composing an ode to the seasons while walking in leaf-laden woods in spring.

Aldous Huxley once wrote: "Experience is not a matter of having actually swum the Hellespont, or danced with the dervishes, or slept in a doss-house. It is a matter of sensibility and intuition, of seeing and hearing the significant things, of paying attention at the right moments, of understanding and coordinating. Experience is not what happens to a [person]; it is what a [person] does with what happens to him [or her]." I have often used those words with students wanting to write.

In this book of essays and poems drawn from her own God-quest, Joanne offers the reader treasures she has gleaned about the mystery of godliness. She reveals what she has done with her life. She examines ordinary events of life and shows how they become for her a step in this journey. She explores her own inner being and shares her thoughts in the kind of poetry that leaves one wishing for more.

The reader savors the unforgettable memory of a grandfather and his homespun piety. Joanne makes herself vulnerable as she expresses thoughts on the poverty of her time-poor generation, and on the tension between her roles as homemaker, career woman, and writer. She takes us along with her as she and her family volunteer to repair damaged homes with Mennonite Disaster Service.

Joanne openly mourns the lack of the arts in worship. Yet on the other hand, she praises God for the support of friends and family and God's presence during a serious accident involving herself and family members. Marital intimacies and family friendships, vacations, poverty, the push of modern technology, war—all are grist for her mill.

Readers will find this a thoughtful, sensitively written album of one writer's reflections, revealing the beauty of the ordinary, the truth hidden in small events of life, and the joy and pain of being human. She is not one to offer platitudinous answers but invites the reader to live the troubling questions with her. What shines through is a dedication to family, a longing for harmony in relationships, and a love of language. She is a wordsmith.

Her hope is that someone else may build something new out of her imagery even as she has been nurtured by the great metaphors of the Bible: beating swords into plowshares, preaching good news, proclaiming freedom to the captives—and always in the background, the illuminating image of Zion, the New Jerusalem.

—*Katie Funk Wiebe*
*Wichita, Kansas*

*Acknowledgments*

THIS, MY FIRST BOOK, reveals my exploration of several forms of the essay and some of my first poetry. Many of these pieces were originally written as class assignments at Malone College. Others are adapted from journal entries or from editorials written for *Ohio Evangel,* or from earlier published writings.

Many instructed me in my craft—tutored me in the writer's art. In the beginning I was encouraged in news and feature writing by Pat Besancon, then the area desk editor at *The Daily Record* of Wooster, Ohio.

David E. Hostetler, editor at Mennonite Publishing House, took a special interest in helping me develop the first articles I submitted to *Purpose* and *Christian Living.*

Another mentor, Katie Funk Wiebe, is the subject of one of the essays in this book. I will always be grateful for her friendship. She is the one who suggested to me that a book is simply a series of articles.

I am indebted to several faculty members at Malone College. My communication arts study, directed by Dr. Kim Phipps, my academic advisor, generated ideas for many of the pieces in this book. Special thanks go to Dale King, for whom I first wrote six of these essays. His random list of sixty-five rhetorical devices was a fascinating discovery. I was instructed by the required readings of classical literature (read aloud onto a tape) and his selection of contemporary writings. He is also responsible for adding to my vocabulary a score of words or more!

My critic Martha Rodak will not have to wait until I'm famous to be remembered. Her enthusiasm for my journal and her helpful critique of my assignments opened new vistas. Her excellent introduction to creative writing was indispensable. She left her door open to me after final grades were posted, reading this manuscript and offering helpful critique over Durango stew and cheese dip.

S. David Garber was on the staff of Ohio Conference when I began working as editor of *Ohio Evangel.* His encouragement then meant much to me. Now, as my book editor, his enthusiastic correspondence after my initial query kept me working.

I deeply appreciate the care of my writing prayer partner, Celia Lehman. She has been there with understanding, giving her support and encouragement as only one of like mind and interests could do.

Finally, I thank my family. Ralph, my husband, believed in my gift as a writer before I believed. His ideas and encouragement keep me learning and growing. Ralph and our children, Jeremy and Laura, ate convenience foods when the Muse made cooking inconvenient; attended impromptu poetry readings at the kitchen counter; and cheered each success. I am also indebted to my parents, Melvin and Pauline Horst, who nurtured creativity in each of their three daughters, producing a musician, an artist, and a writer.

Among my greatest treasures, I count the love and friendship of those mentioned above and many others.

—*Joanne Lehman*

# *Prologue*

GROWING UP, early on I developed a love affair with words—spoken and written. Telling stories was a way of life, and reading stories was a passion. Words of stories, hymns, poems, and sermons blazed a pathway for my faith. Simply for the love of hearing words, I formed them into sentences when no one would hear them, and I wrote volumes in my mind, without a pen or pencil ever recording them. I was the preacher when we played church. Words made music for me when I found joy in pouring them on paper and felt the rhythm of writing flowing from my pen.

However, I learned also that words manipulate, intimidate, infuriate, sedate. Too often in the church, words take a numbing pietistic turn—in the worst sense of that word. I write here of piety in the best sense, the devoted inner life—this collection of conscious and subconscious living, which welds thought and action. Here I offer traces of one disciple's treasure—present in simple things as well as in the large events of life, an elemental spirituality.

My quest for God leads me to the commonplace. For here in questions posed by everyday life, the Holy Spirit walks with me and shares life's simple joys, sorrows, fears, and all human experience and emotions. Such spiritual awareness creates a faith that becomes something beyond an intellectual exercise or a segment of life. This wholeness that embraces holiness is a form of prayer.

Holiness is a secret part of the disciple even without my awareness—even when one "slip[s] off life's little bucky horse," as E. B. White once put it. It transcends words, both for description here and in the practice of this prayer which really is a kind of *living*. I don't think of this prayer as something done on my knees. It is a walk. A total emphasis of life. A focal point. A center. It is done in isolation. I have learned it on my own. It is not easy to mark it out—exactly what it is or how it works—a relationship of the self with the divine, an ethereal existence. What could be more isolationist than this?

But where does this isolation lead? Only back to others—but by God's grace, back as someone different, renewed in mind and heart for more—a circle of hope for living the faith here where I'm presently planted. I treasure the poetry in my disciplehood and feel compelled to challenge silence and frame my faith with words. Like the romantics of the Victorian era, I write my life on journal pages and paste in scraps of prose that capture my attention. Here I trace life's treasure, not as the scientist or theologue, but as one who sings the words and despises skipping verses.

# Hymns
## to
## Piety

# *Stewardship*

## CALLING HOURS

People with canes
walk slowly
wear hearing aids
Sunday clothes
pungent polyester suits
rolled-up, bobby-pinned
blue and yellow white hair.
Thick black handbags
sensible shoes
gnarled rheumatic hands
grip memorial leaflets.
Youhavemysympathy.
mechanical voices
pumping hands
how we're related
don't know *them* either.
Thankyouforcoming.
Relief, it's over.
Now the casket
Why stand so long looking?
Grandpa isn't
here a nutshell
dried cornstalk.
Who could know
what to say?

# The Bishop's Treasure

GRANDPA REUBEN is gone now; Ralph's grandpa, dear to me as my own grandpas, but different. Reuben Hofstetter was a bishop. But not the stern dictatorial type I've heard about. We called him Grandpa Reuben for our children, to distinguish him from their other grandpas.

He was a round, jolly bishop, and even when he wore a plain coat—the Mennonite clerical collar—he could never conceal a certain exuberance, a habit he had of dashing humor into conversation at unexpected places. Grandpa Reuben became a deacon, then a preacher, and a bishop back in the days when leaders were chosen by lot. He was unschooled, and his sermons were long and rambling and unpolished. His prayers were equally long and rambling; but what is important is that love for his flock shone through them.

In the end he finally lived in a nursing home for a few years, his mind gone and his body wasted. I'm ashamed to say that I didn't visit him much there. But memories of him as he was in his early nineties are still fresh in my mind. I turn to my journal and to newspaper clippings—I wrote a feature piece about his life for his ninetieth birthday. But it is a journal entry which reminds me of something that happened between us. I wrote of one poignant moment: at the auction when his things were sold. He attended and was still of sound mind then.

Yet he and his second wife, Ida, had decided to move in with Ida's son, who would care for them.

As a young woman with a growing family, I was still longing to collect things for my own nest. I couldn't imagine putting my things up for auction and then standing there watching, making small talk. But the twinkle was still in the bishop's eye. His old voice was foggy as his eyes met mine: "Can I interest you in anything here?"

"I'll probably buy something tomorrow; I don't know what. . . ." I glanced at the oak library table and the glass-front bookcase. The straight chairs, old lamps, or the blanket chest—any of these would fit into our newly finished family room. I noted that there weren't many old crocks or picture frames or iron beds; the farm had been sold years ago. And there were no boxes of old jewelry!

• • •

My thoughts reach out to Grandpa Reuben. In spite of the twinkle and the ninety-three-year-old humor, it must hurt to see all your earthly possessions strewn on tables. These household items must bring back memories: the chairs you sat in, the dishes you ate from, the odds and ends, accumulated over a lifetime. No doubt there's a story behind each one. You say you can't remember much anymore.

Your things, products of blended households, look worn—useless clutter here. I'm embarrassed for you to have to see them like this. ("What will you give me for this old vaporizer? . . . Still works good. . . . Who'll give me a dollar to start us off?")

But you are a bishop emeritus, and you don't need all of this anymore. You have your sweater, your cane, your glasses, and Bible. You have a bed and a rocking chair and someone who loves you to take care of your needs. You don't need mops and knives and muffin tins and good china and worn-out throw rugs.

For years you worked in your study at the sturdy oak library table, surrounded by shelves of books. Books that have your name on the flyleaf. It's been a long time since you've read some of them. Some, I suppose, you've never read. Now they're stacked in boxes and soon people will be pawing through them, hungry for a piece of the bishop's spirituality—as if it could somehow be absorbed through the yellow pages and dark, greasy cloth bindings.

The special old books are in a narrow box: leather-bound German Bibles. Hymnbooks with metal clasps. The print is flowing and lovely to look at. The paper is fine. But I can't read German. Members of the historical society stop by to put in a request for items for the archives. They look hungrily at the book published in Basel, 1811. "How much would we dare spend, do you think?" I hear them whispering to each other. No frakturs in the books, they say. That's a disappointment.

• • •

Is this all there is? A lifetime lined up around the yard. Here we have no continuing city, but our citizenship is in heaven. . . . I recall the day I walked beside Grandpa Reuben in the church cemetery after a funeral. "This is my spot," he said cheerily, staking out his claim with the end of his cane, "unless the Lord returns first." The rubber tip pointed up from the sod. "Then we who are alive and remain will be caught up in the air with him. So shall we ever be with the Lord!" Definitely a pre-millennialist! And there was that twinkle again. Somehow it didn't matter that we were talking about death. Earth seemed so temporary right then.

The evening before the auction, sitting in my living room surrounded with my own that often seem so precious, I suddenly knew what of Grandpa Reuben's things I most wanted. And the things I wanted couldn't be placed on an auction block. I longed for the intangible qualities of life, as he lived it. These have nothing to do with possessions. I'd make a bid for that twinkle in his eye in spite of sorrow; his ability always to see the good in other people; the gracious and simple life, lived out in humility of character; his gift for sharing Scripture at a moment's notice, with or without the Book; the gentle way he shepherded his flock and sheltered them in the sheepfold of his prayers. In this category, my possessions seemed shabby.

Our Sunday school teacher had described Grandpa Reuben's bequest a few weeks earlier at the end of a lively discussion of spiritual gifts. "I think of our bishop," he said, summing up the lesson. "Reuben wasn't a great preacher. He wasn't a great scholar. He wasn't a great counselor. He wasn't a great writer. But he took the few talents he had and marched into 1 Corinthians 13. He understood that the greatest gift is love. How many times he stood in front of the congregation and said, with deep sincerity, 'God bless you! I love you all!' "

• • •

As chaff to the wind, the tin pie pans, old songbooks, worn chairs, and chenille bedspreads will scatter across the community. Glassware will be placed on someone else's shelf, to both burden and delight during spring cleaning—perhaps to be auctioned off again some other year.

I suppose it's inevitable, this collecting. A shelf. A drawer. A jar. A chest. A book with a latch on the covers. We want something to call our own. We stake a claim in the sod, gather trinkets, write our names in books, and leave a marker to show where we've been.

I paid a terrible price for my copy of Grandpa Reuben's *Martyrs Mirror*, although it was not the older edition. Not a few people were bidding against me. Later I found several pressed flowers between the pages. I also got a cheap though unabridged, tattered copy of *Pilgrim's Progress* and one of those hickory rockers (not an antique) popular in our part of the country. Oh, yes, I collected a few other items that went cheap—a broken stand which I painted and put on my back porch, a pretty lamp with a frayed cord which didn't work and ended up in the Goodwill box, and an old desk lamp, repaired, which I still use.

I have one other thing which I think of as Grandpa Reuben's: a pulpit chair that someone bought at a church auction and later bequeathed to Ralph and me. It's an odd thing really, homemade and heavy and large and wide, with short legs (unlike present leaders, all the early pastors at Kidron were short). The chair is surprisingly comfortable.

I upholstered it in a modern pink-and-blue tapestry, and it now sits in the corner of my office—the guest chair of a Mennonite conference editor. It's a conversation starter, and people enjoy sitting in it. They're surprised how comfortable it really is. Soon they relax and begin to tell me about church life, about their lives. And somehow Grandpa Reuben's legacy lives on, his peculiar brand of homespun piety. In odd moments I can still sometimes catch an inner vision of the twinkle in the bishop's eye.

## RETREAT

Elijah, mental martyr
fearful, fleeing,
exhausted, alone.
Caving in to despair.
Looking for God
in burning bushes,
earthquakes, rushing winds.
But God speaks quietly
and feeds the fugitive
and urges sleep.

# *At Elder's House,*
# *Pretending to Be Monastic*

PULLING THE STICKERS from my pants after a walk in the woods, I got to thinking how nature is so full of unrealized potential. Each sticker is a seed, yet many will never germinate and grow. The dying leaves swirl around me, another testimony to the temporariness of life and the haphazard way it seems to work itself out for the individual.

I nearly stepped on a dead opossum lying on the trail, the fur torn off his side. How did he die? And why? He is only one tiny infinitesimal part of a very large whole. Will anyone care, except that his corpse blocks the path?

I marvel at the gigantic brown oak leaves, scattered on the trail. A few weeks ago they were living, green; now they are dead and I walk on them. Is there one to keep? But none quite pleases me.

The giant oak itself is a comfort to me, though. This oak, where I sit, rises out of the side of a massive rock, as if in competition with it. Or perhaps, better, a living testimony to the sandstone platform it shelters. The leaves die and swirl down. The oak lives on.

A prickly pear reminds me of the crown of thorns. The tree's blood courses through its veins. It is almost November, and grapevines cheer me. Their twisted branches spiral up the tree trunks in the woods. The new cultivated grapevines are still so tiny.

I think I understand why the owners planted them here on the hillside of this fledgling hermitage. "I am the vine, you are the branches. Abide in me, and you *will* bring forth fruit. . . . This is the blood of my covenant, poured out for many. . . . Except a grain of wheat fall into the ground and die, it cannot bear fruit."

There is an inexplicable wholeness here in this death trap we call life. But you will not discover its meaning by concentrating on the individual. How can one little sticker seed, one tarnished oak leaf, or one dead opossum contribute, or have contributed, anything of value? Not as an individual certainly. . . .

It is October 20 something, and I am entering a new phase of life. Last year was terrible. Everything began to look up sometime during the summer. Until then, I failed somehow to understand how unbalanced I was, so tired, angry, troubled, paranoid, and somehow wayward. My explanations for this dry season yielded many answers: too many people, a ghost from the past, the stress of raising children, too many demands and responsibilities.

In a sense, perhaps it was a death, pride falling off, even a period of regeneration. Now this pause at the crossroad signals a new direction. A turn in the road heralds a new outlook. This time I vow not to be so wrapped up in myself, nor so idealistic in my expectations of others. I desire to move beyond a self-realization, self-gratification, self-actualization pattern of living to a clearer picture of a whole—a whole that sees self as a minute part, not the center of the universe. It should be possible to move beyond grandiose ideas of the self to a place where greatness and grace blend to create wholeness in the person. Maybe nature gives the proper perspective. . . .

• • •

We are at the Elder's House, pretending we are monastic. At first we looked on it as a cheap getaway weekend. It is a kind of Christian's Walden Pond, and there was no real reason to go anywhere else. (Now that I'm here, I know I should never have let go of the childhood habit of woods walking and contemplation.)

It is my second time at this retreat, and already I feel at home. It is right somehow to be away from everything, in silence and solitude. The *shoulds* and *oughts* recede into the background and make me question why any of my life is as complicated as it is.

Why, for instance, do we rake leaves? At home we would be raking. We came here to escape. The best thing here is silence. I crave silence. At home there is always a TV or radio going somewhere in the house, sometimes more than one.

Clutter, at home, has a vague tyranny about it. When things are out of place, I'm out of sorts, or I think someone else might be. My life is pressed through a nozzle, like water through the garden hose. It comes out with explosive force, attacking defined areas of clutter while others are neglected. I like the clutter and randomness of this place, with the weeds, piles of rocks, brush, stacked-up slabs of wood.

Is there something that breeds unhealthiness in a life that is too orderly? Does one ever really get all one's "ducks in a row"? Or is that a myth that leads us away from a more healthy truth, that all of life is probably

31

somewhat messy and there's nothing too saintly about keeping everything in perfect order.

With the saints of old, I aim to sit and listen more. My appetites shut down, sitting here listening to nature, to the God of nature. How many of our modern patterns would be eliminated if we were to practice regularly the habits of the ancients! Jogging and exercise machines offset rich foods which we consume in an effort to find some inner comfort for a hunger we never took the time to identify. We were so busy running from place to place and thing to thing.

Could our hunger be for rest, solitude, nature, silence, and time? Could jogging tracks and exercise programs be superfluous for saints?

Perhaps it is not too late to reinstate the childhood custom of woods walking and contemplation. Until coming here, I'd nearly forgotten what a woods can do for the spirit, or how a grapevine can speak to a soul.

## CIRCUS PEANUTS

A heavy, fluted crystal
    candy dish
    rested on a shelf
    near the cellar door.
Grandma didn't have her teeth in;
    whistled under her breath
    as she glided by, a billow
    of cotton housedress.

Listening on the scratchy wool carpet
    for the clink.
    Orange marshmallow
    dissolves quietly
    without trouble or mess.

Circus peanuts are ninety-nine cents
    at K-Mart. Forgetting
    the taste we buy and eat
    remembering only
    childhood Grandma softness.

But they are too sweet
    and not good. Why did
    she buy them anyway?

To savor a sweet sale
    fill an empty crystal dish
    or perchance, conceive a
    sugary soft spun poem
    of marshmallow memory.

# A Piety Examined

> Lift up your heads, ye mighty gates,
>   Behold the King of glory waits;
> The King of kings is drawing near,
>   the Savior of the world is here;
> Life and salvation doth He bring,
>   Wherefore rejoice and gladly sing. . . .*

GRANDPA MARTIN died when he was ninety-eight; I inherited one of his hymnbooks. It speaks to me from tattered, yellow pages of uncommon devotion and articulated faith. Even when he was in his nineties, Grandpa used to sing, unconcerned about his voice cracking from age. He sang at home, to himself, to God. If you listened for it, every Sunday morning you could hear his voice above the others in the Leetonia Mennonite Church, where he attended for his entire life.

When, as a fifth grader, I finally admitted defeat and gave up on the piano, Grandpa Martin was the one who said at Sunday dinner, "Joanne doesn't need the piano; her voice is her instrument." With that pronouncement, Grandpa pointed me toward the hymns that now pronounce *my* faith.

In many homes today, the hymnal is buried in a musty piano bench, if they even own a personal copy. Sincere Christians search the shelves of religious bookstores for "a good devotional book" or "some inspirational reading." Meanwhile, in the humble hymnbook, poetry which has survived centuries waits to bring us into the presence of a God of love, beauty, and mystery.

In many churches the great hymns of antiquity are being replaced by catchy, repetitious choruses. This new church music, say those who promote it, makes it easier for visitors and new members to join in worship. Worship should be easy, even effortless, these people seem to imply.

Other worshipers shun the staid old hymns in favor of a more expressive style of singing. They encourage people to sing with their eyes closed and hands raised, or to clap and sway to bouncy rhythms. (For my part, I am content with an active *mind* during worship.)

To be sure, there are good reasons to experiment with new music and to include variety in our worship services. I admit that, like my grandpa before me, I too have sung my share of choruses, gospel songs, praise songs, and Scripture songs; and I enjoy them. For one thing, they are easy to sing—something like setting the cruise control and heading down a four-lane highway.

In contrast, singing a Bach chorale is like backing an eighteen-wheeler into an alley. My mind is filled with imagery and borne aloft as I reach out to God with meaning-laden vocabulary that tries a thousand ways ("Oh, for a thousand tongues to sing my great Redeemer's praise . . .") to describe, to glorify, to call upon an indescribable God. I measure my breath, stretching toward the final chord in one unbroken phrase ("I'll praise my Maker with my breath, / And when my voice is lost in death . . ."). Praise is sacrifice and requires work, energy, and attention.

The rich poetry of traditional hymns, which have stood the test of time, affords the best that wordsmiths ever crafted to honor and worship our Savior. In 1848 Oliver Wendell Holmes drew a line to connect the Jesus of the apostle John's Revelation with Mary's beloved rabbi. What a gift this verse!

> Lord of all being, throned afar,
> Thy glory flames from sun and star;
> Center and soul of every sphere,
> Yet to each loving heart how near!

It *is* true, as the modern chorus says, "God is so good . . . (repeat 3x); God's so good to me." But to my way of thinking, the hymn writer with these words said more and said it better:

> Immortal, invisible, God only wise,
> In light inaccessible hid from our eyes,
> Most blessed, most glorious, the Ancient of Days,
> Almighty, victorious Thy great name we praise. . . .

What a wonderful discovery: the name of the hymn tune is "Joanna!"

For those who seek a life of holiness in the Spirit, what better way to begin a new day than by singing the ritual call to worship with which I grew up?

> Breathe on me, Breath of God,
> Fill me with life anew,
> That I may love what Thou dost love,
> And do what Thou wouldst do.

Some people praise the overhead projector for freeing hands that lifted heavy hymnals. I say the weight in my hand is worth it for the wings these words give my spirit. While I recognize the value of simplicity in many areas of life, I personally question the worth, to God or to ourselves, of any song made up of a seven-word vocabulary. And I wonder why we need an overhead projector to help us remember those words.

The extravagant language of many old hymns becomes imprinted on your memory once you've sung them a few times with the intellect engaged. Wrap your tongue and mind around the rich poetry written by Joseph Addison in 1712, and you will never again be speechless when viewing God's creation. The words come back to haunt you at dusk as you observe a glorious sunset. No need to search for words of your own.

> The spacious firmament on high,
>     With all the blue ethereal sky,
> And spangled heav'ns a shining frame,
>     Their great Original proclaim.
> Th'unwearied sun, from day to day,
>     Does his Creator's power display,
> And publishes, to every land,
>     The work of an almighty hand.

The repetitious pabulum of popular gospel choruses will never mine the depth of passion nor call forth repentance as ably or as simply as does Synesius of Cyrene from the fifth century:

> Lord Jesus, think on me,
>     And purge away my sin;

> From earth-born passions set me free,
> And make me pure within.

> Lord Jesus, think on me,
> Nor let me go astray;
> Through darkness and perplexity
> Point Thou the heav'nly way.

No ringing joy bells of heaven here; only the solemn petition of a sinner caught in "darkness and perplexity," "with care and woe oppressed." I should sing this prayer every day. Is it a commentary on our modern-day spiritual sensitivity that this ancient hymn is one of our neglected treasures?

Even the "me-centered" gospel hymns often wear thin: "I've found a Friend, O such a Friend . . ." "I will sing the wondrous story . . ." "I will sing of my Redeemer . . ." "I am Thine O Lord . . ." These and many similar songs have easy and breezy answers. Their lilting melodies obscure the often solemn nature of an authentic Christian experience. In times of spiritual anguish, I turn to treasure:

> Jesus, priceless treasure,
> Source of purest pleasure,
> Truest friend to me;
> Long my heart hath panted,
> Till it well-nigh fainted,
> Thirsting after Thee.
> Thine I am, O spotless Lamb,
> I will suffer naught to hide Thee,
> Ask for naught beside Thee.

In Thine arm I rest me;
   Foes who would molest me
    Cannot reach me here.
Though the earth be shaking,
   Every heart be quaking,
    Jesus calms my fear;
Sin and hell in conflict fell
   With their heaviest storms assail me:
    Jesus will not fail me.

Doyle Preheim, professor of music at Goshen College, says that one of music's gifts to us is the message of humility. Perfection in music cannot be achieved. Some object to my preference for difficult music and my taste for texts requiring the exercise of intellectual muscle. I remind such that praise should be sacrifice. Sincere worship may require more work, energy, and attention than most of us now give to a three-stanza hymn during the Sunday morning worship hour. To experience joy from our musical experience in worship, we need not be competent musicians. Instead, we must endeavor to join mind and heart to One whose being is beyond human comprehension.

This human journey, our attempt to reach out and touch God, however inept and stumbling it may be, will become meaningful in its own right. A few years back, at a conference for leaders of urban churches, Gerald Hughes, the minister of music at Lee Heights Community Church in Cleveland, taught us an old but unfamiliar hymn from African-American culture. No overhead projector was summoned, and no song sheets were rattled down the aisles. Humbly, with an unassuming manner, Gerry "lined out" each verse, and we echoed him. Although I become nervous when asked to learn a new hymn without seeing the notes, Gerry's creamy baritone soon calmed me. I trusted him as he led me through the winding, unfamiliar text and tune.

My attention was riveted to the words of the hymn as each stanza revealed another dimension of divine guidance. Suddenly we had come to the end of the hymn. I felt a surge of spiritual energy and knew that I had truly worshiped. Only later did I understood how Gerald's leadership had been a metaphor for the hymn's refrain: "Lead me, O Lord, lead me." When the words of a good hymn lead us, we can trust the path.

John, the great New Testament mystic, tells us that "the Word became flesh and lived among us, and we have seen his glory" (John 1:14). Surely such a God, a God whose Son is "the Word," would be honored by our repeating the rich poetic language of the great hymns of the church. These words could be a means by which we comprehend more fully the mystery of the incarnation. How can we be satisfied to mindlessly *repeat* the words we sing from our hymnals? Might the hymnbook, thoughtfully appropriated, ignite a spiritual fire again within our souls? How can any Christian not revel in this opportunity to receive aid in trying to describe the indescribable?

---

* Hymn texts are from *The Mennonite Hymnal* (Scottdale, Pa.: Herald Press, 1969); used by permission.

## BACKROAD PHILOSOPHER

Suffer me not to love the rose,
proper in the rose patch
budding, all secure
in flower promise
indebted to the
visionless gardener
duty-bound, staked up
thatched down, pruned, guarded
for the flower to be.

But revel, my love
in backroad bouquets!
dull skies
weathered fences
frame wild beauty
can't contain it.
Defiant blossoms
shout glory
mock overcast October.

Rejoice my soul in weedness!
Purple thistle blossoms
stands of goldenrod
and royal carrot laces.

Blue sailors sing on naked stalks
and tell of vanished daisies
Revel, yes, in this:
The random winds of weed-dom
sing wild Creator praises.

# Senses, the Arts, and Worship

SOMETIMES I LONG to be Episcopalian, kneeling on padded kneeling rails, chanting centuries-old prayers. I yearn to be called to worship by steeple chimes to a sanctuary filled with visions of shimmering saints with sunlight streaming through their halos.

But centuries ago, Anabaptists rejected the excessive pomp and pageantry of state religion and the accompanying injustice to the peasantry. They opted instead for simplicity of word and deed. Some say that the remaining present-day formal and traditional worship is shallow, empty, and dead. Yet I sometimes feel *my own* tradition is feeble and unsatisfying.

Someone once remarked that the most complete worship must have been possible in a Gothic cathedral of the Middle Ages. All the senses were called into service. Fingers counted rosary beads while knees and elbows pressed against stone floors and smooth wood. Incense wafted over and around the worshiper, while the eyes feasted on stained glass, lighted only by sunlight and candles. Ears absorbed biblical poetry, the chanted mass, often set to music. Wordless music somehow found a way into the soul, and the tongue tasted the wafer and the pungent grape.

Words printed on paper were the property of priests. Common people came to know the truth through ear, eye, taste, touch, and smell. We pity pre-Reformation Christians and speak with awe of Gutenberg, who put the printed page within the reach of spiritually malnourished masses. We never consider that we might have lost something they had.

One worshiper told me he had experimented with attending church "paperless." He determined to worship for a time without the printed word and the distraction and self-absorption it can bring. He sang from memory, listened to Scripture without following in his Bible, and shunned the bulletin. Is there anything in our Sunday morning service for the illiterate seeker or the learning-disabled Christian? What would be there for *us* if we put aside our endless paper and its diversion?

We are a people of the word, perhaps almost to exclusion. We worship with the intellect and eschew our feelings and resident intuition. In our places of worship, what preaches through the sense of sight? Artful arrangements of plants and flowers speak of warmth, care, and hope. Landscaped entrances, inviting foyers, and cozy Sunday school rooms are all ways to speak God's love. Candles share the light; banners declare the truth; lace would not be out of place.

"I don't mean to be dramatic, but . . . ," the pastor says. And I beg, "Why not be dramatic?" Worship is theater. Not that worship is a "show," but theater by its true definition involves the audience as well as those on stage. The language of worship captures and carries worshipers through a communal event which shapes the way they respond to God. A good theater audience breathes, sighs, and shifts in their seats in unison. They discover a mysterious oneness that transmits energy to feet that lead

out the door and onto the street after the last curtain call. Days after attending good theater, the recollection of emotion lingers, bringing back that energy. We long to return again and again to the theater, and if we cannot return bodily, we return again within our spirit.

Unfortunately, the "Jesus Is the Answer" bumper-sticker approach to worship is what we often serve up on Sunday morning. Instead, people need help connecting that "answer" to life's pressing questions of the moment. We forget too often that the grandest revelations are not always trumpeted from the pulpit but are born gently, breathed in through the senses, heard in the still, small voice, or felt in the presence of Christ among his people.

Worship should not be allowed to become a spectator sport. Anything worship leaders can do to capture and hold attention and encourage variety is a welcome addition. In so doing, worship becomes true theater. Our pastor, Bill Detweiler, has roamed to the balcony during the sermon, where he preached from the ledge. He sometimes brings props and tells personal stories or quotes poetry. Once during a Lenten service, our hearts froze within us as crucifixion nails were driven into a plank in an adjoining room.

Whether it is a fast-paced contemporary piece of music, a trumpet fanfare, or the sudden appearance of a clown or an "angel," the unexpected invites me to join the worship drama. I am jolted out of my drowsy distraction and required to make some sense of what is happening.

On a dark December evening, our congregation sits packed together on the pews in expectation. The minister of music, dressed in burlap and swinging a lantern, comes down the aisle, singsonging the message of John the Baptist. The Christmas story comes alive through music and spectacle, rich in meaning when actors are my fellow members. Gigantic camels cut from cardboard crates are painted with such whimsical expressions that I almost expect them to speak. Banners shout the incarnation.

Despite our need to experience worship with the senses, the church often holds its artists at arm's length or ignores their work entirely. The arts were a casualty of the Reformation, and still in many Protestant traditions, we deny them legitimation.

For too long we've relied on sermonizing, theorizing, and moralizing. In the sixteenth century, Ulrich Zwingli whitewashed murals and removed instruments, candles, statues—everything but the word—because worship had been cluttered and adulterated by objects.

But the time has now come for us cautiously to begin reclaiming what was always ours. Promising signs are on the horizon. Christian artists are banding together to bring about a revival of storytelling and to herald the advent of visual media. The arts are beginning to dance freely among us once more.

The Judeo-Christian worship tradition is founded on story, hymn, dance, chant, and psalm. Through these we engage the imagination, subdue the intellect for a time, and experience true religion, which nurtures faith-needs of the heart. Imagery, symbolism, and rhythm lie buried here within us, waiting to be discovered anew. As we regain our art, we may also rediscover the practice of the true worship we had, for some time, thought was lost forever.

## WINTER OF BACKYARD CONTENTMENT

Brown gray waiting
dreaming for the
chiming clock
church bells
a simple yes.

Sleeping bulbs
under damp leaf blankets
snuggle in crystallized
earth expecting Spring.

Time wouldn't move
except clocks tick
cycle in confidence
through Westminster notes
of hope accompaniment
for an invisible
daffodil chorus
awaiting the downbeat.

# God of the Calendar and Daytimer

ACCORDING TO MY CALENDAR, in the past month I attended two school open houses, one parent-teacher conference, and an elementary school parents' meeting; helped plan and host a fortieth wedding anniversary celebration for my parents; met a friend for lunch; hosted a progressive supper; attended two sessions of the Lay Academy and an all-day seminar in Columbus; baby-sat for another friend; gave a craft demonstration at a homemakers' meeting; sewed a vest and a panda-bear costume; went on an afternoon outing with my daughter; took my son and his friend to the mall; exercised at least four times a week; introduced my fifth-grade Sunday school class to *Martyrs Mirror* and explored with them the lives of Samuel, Saul, David, and Nathan.

I also went out to lunch with my husband, painted my living room walls, had lunch with my co-workers, tried a new recipe, invited guests for Sunday dinner, perused the church periodicals, and read aloud to the family. This log of activities doesn't include the routine housework, after-school chats with the kids, driving to lessons and activities, shopping and errands, and my regular though part-time job.

A list of accomplishments like that ought to give me a sense of satisfaction, but it doesn't—quite. I can make an equally long list of things I could (or should?)

have done. I fend off guilt for all I left undone. I have no time now to sort out whether this is true or false guilt. That too will have to wait.

I missed two meetings in the Lay Academy series; I missed the Renewal Conference meetings that took place less than one mile from my home. I didn't attend a "Calling and Caring" workshop at our church—despite my earlier aid in promoting the concept. I didn't attend the stewardship workshop that Ralph helped lead, and we missed the MEDA meeting. I didn't go to the chapel dedication at Camp Luz or to the WMSC retreat.

I also didn't write in my journal, write letters (although I did send several cards), or compose any articles. This month I didn't read any books (except the one I read aloud). I didn't bake any cookies, rake any leaves, or plant any spring bulbs.

 Life seems to whirl faster and faster and, for most of us, the church is no refuge from the chaos. Year by year more activities seem to be added to the church calendar. Psychologist and humorist Emerson Lesher says that some small groups have been known to take several hours to coordinate their schedules and plan for the next meeting. But that didn't seem so funny when our small group was trying to find a weekend for a camping trip!

Some of us drop exhausted at the end of a hectic day, only to get up early the next morning to type minutes or attend a breakfast planning session. Ironically, the speakers at the meetings we plan always seem to be talking about silence, nurturing the inner spirit, or going "into the desert alone with God."

Is there any way out of this thing that writer Ralph Keyes calls "timelock"? Of 450 people who filled out his

questionnaire, 57 percent said their lives had grown busier during the last year. More than half agreed with this statement: "There aren't enough hours in the day to do everything I have to do." Keyes believes that our time-saving devices have contributed to the stepped-up pace of our lives—those cordless and car phones, laptop computers, and the many household appliances we now consider necessities.

We expect more of ourselves than ever before. "Only by slowing down and pruning our schedules can we reclaim the most valuable thing we own: our time," says Keyes. It is not an easy or desirable task. We resist.

[Many years ago, both daily life and church life were lived more simply.]While browsing through historical records, I noticed that one church canceled Sunday school during the winter months. Many churches scheduled services only twice a month. I wondered then if I was born too late.(Sometimes I long to live in olden days. Year by year more things are added. Nothing ever seems to get subtracted.

Grandma sat on the front porch and shelled peas. Grandpa rested the horses at the end of the furrow. Both worked in silence, listening to the sounds of nature or to the inner voice. Perhaps they hummed a hymn, prayed for a family member, or did whatever they did to get ready for those sermons they preached on Sunday without sermon notes.)

We, the grandchildren, microwave frozen peas in their plastic pouch and watch television news while we load the dishwasher. Our minds and hands are full of ourselves. And on the bottom line, time is money and money is success.

( Today our lives are ruled by penciled reminders on calendars and Daytimers carried close to our hearts. It is an honor of highest rank to be *inked* into another's Daytimer. When we do finally meet with friends, more often than not, conversation turns to our mutually busy schedules. My friend hasn't had one evening at home this week. I mourn her loss.)

"I am not busy!" declares pastor Paul Versluis. We

hearers gasp. He tells a group of pastors that "busy" is a four-letter word, a way of distancing ourselves from others. Indeed, why bother busy people with my joys, my needs? Would they have time to listen if I did?

Increasingly, I think, we contour life around schedules and tasks instead of around people or our desire for communion with God. Church life is filled with committee meetings and task forces. Church music and other elements of worship are expected to be of professional quality. We meet God at retreats because "time-lock" warps each ordinary day.

Sabbath moments are irreclaimable; worship, forgotten. Versluis speaks of "domestic piety"—seeing God and being attentive to God in all things. Yes, it is difficult, but we can choose to live deliberately as pilgrims in a society consumed by its consumption and influenced by affluence on display. We can choose—at least for long moments of our lives now and again, maybe finally daily, even hourly—to become "not busy," even when doing God's work.

The frightening thing about being "not busy" is the thought of all those things I've missed—the meetings, retreats, courses, workshops—endless possibilities surround me. All are good, and I don't want to choose. I must somehow extinguish this idea I cling to so passionately: that my value to God and to others, even my very own self-worth, lies in what I do—how many meetings I attend, how many church committees I sit on, how many workshops I lead—even how many kindnesses I perform for my family.

Whether it is better to do, or to be: that is the question. "Be still and know that I am God." This is Sabbath.

The cessation of commotion when God invades my Daytimer and I choose to stop everything in order to become.)

## STABLE THINKING

The lantern swinging overhead catches cobwebs
   looped like so much Christmas tinsel
      from the rafters of the stable.
         Children and grownups gather in the barn cellar
            warmly wrapped, we squirm on scratchy bales
               of straw.

Chipper, the floppy-eared goat
   Teases and distracts us. A black and white cat
      resists being held captive in our crèche.
         Cows breathe new meaning into the words
            of an old carol—the cattle are lowing.

We shiver on the straw and listen
   to the old, old words—
      Mary . . . laid him in a manger.
         In a barn we ponder the meaning of Christmas
         and try to ignore bone-chilling cold.

It seeps in around the corners of old stone walls
   and rattles the chains of our subconscious.
      Until now, we kept forgetting . . .
         Christmas is cold and uncomfortable, Jesus . . .
         at least it was for you.

# *Waiting for Christmas*

THE CURIOSITY that currently fuels my interest in journalism got me into trouble as a child. This was especially true around Christmastime. My parents used to wrap our gifts and place them under the tree several days (or was it weeks?) before Christmas. My sisters and I sat on the floor near the Christmas tree by the hour, shaking the packages that had our names on them, stretching our eyeballs to see through the thin wrapping paper, even picking at the tape until it "accidentally" came loose.

Not only that, I was liberally endowed with intuition but not with a lot of discretion. Often, to my parents' probable disappointment, their eldest daughter was able to identify nearly every gift before untying a single ribbon.

As a parent, I wrap our children's gifts in heavy wrapping paper and camouflage some gifts in different-sized boxes. Hints don't come readily, and there is usually at least one gift that no one could possibly guess. Surprises are part of a good Christmas and are guarded well.

I believe children should learn to wait even though it is often difficult. The message of Advent comes through this living in anticipation, while waiting. Of such a season, our world knows little.

We envy children their enthusiasm for Christmas. Memories of childhood Christmases warm our hearts for a lifetime and create the patterns of expectation for all future celebrations. In the mind's eye, one can still see the Salvation Army woman on the street corner near the five-and-dime—there with her tripod and black kettle, wearing fur-trimmed rubber boots. We hear the bell, ringing and ringing. Most of all, we remember the warm feeling in our hearts when we impulsively gave a few spare coins, believing without a doubt that we'd done our part.

Years later, as adults, we eye with annoyance the locked metal box which now replaces the kettle. The lieutenant or general, or whoever she is, holds the bell with a gloved hand over one side to mute the distraction. One now suspects cold calculation, that she's standing beside the "in" door to get customer's money before it is spent.

As we begin to create Christmas celebrations for our own families, we start to understand the sacrifice and energy it takes—and sometimes we don't get the whole thing right. We want to remain children at Christmas, but it has become impossible.

During the years our young family lived on a shoestring budget, I made Christmas difficult through my compulsion to make gifts, develop unique family traditions, and design a holiday that measured up to the one remembered in embellished memories of my own childhood. I tried valiantly to reproduce the festivity pictured in women's magazines.

As a young homemaker, I filled the days before Christmas with frantic attempts to cram in one more activity, finish one more project, wrap one last present, send one more letter, write one more card, remember one more neighbor with a home-baked gift. A time or so,

much to my embarrassment, I didn't even manage to complete all the gifts I had started.

One year we bought the tallest Christmas tree we could find, only to have all the needles fall off a week later. We even failed to learn the obvious object lesson implied by the experience, that a bigger Christmas is not always better.

When Christmas festivities were over, inevitably a feeling of despair settled in. I was never satisfied with what I had done and never believed I had given enough. By now it was obvious that giving involved more than throwing some spare change into a kettle on a street corner, but my activities did not bring the requisite magical Christmas feelings. Instead, some years I was so exhausted by December 25 that it was a relief for it to be over.

Finally, after several years of this, I began to understand that my motives for these counterfeit Advent activities should be held suspect. Realistic expectations gradually replaced my frantic efforts. The gift of the coming

Christ became my center, not the giving and receiving of gifts. In a sense this gift giving is merely a symbol of God's revelation to us in the form of the Son. What was hidden now appears; the Word becomes flesh and dwells with us.

The commercial Christmas world offers a continuous feast. It has no patience with fasting, waiting, and watching in hope of some future celebration. It beams its unholy noises in our direction, attempting to persuade us, to draw us into its circle and away from the righteous keeping of our sacred festival. Yet wholistic Christianity reminds us that fasting precedes feasting and is its complement. We have a responsibility to choose so much more than foil-wrapped gifts for family and friends. More importantly, we must also choose how we will respond to the messages that encompass us at the height of the commercial year.

Already in October advertisements begin suggesting gifts and bid us look, smell, taste, and touch, rushing us on to revelry with carols tarnished from overuse. All the while, Advent hymns languish, unfamiliar and unsung. The ceaseless whine and hollow jingle of "holiday" Muzak grinds away at our spirits—audible tinsel clinging stubbornly to a false sense of religiosity. The world urges us to bypass preparation of our hearts and concentrate instead on trinkets.

But true religion leads first to the desert: the silent 400 years between Malachi and Matthew, the forty years of Hebrew wilderness wandering, the forty temptation-filled days and nights of Christ, the darkness of Gethsemane. . . . Waiting is the hard lesson of keeping faith despite the odds. Of this kind of waiting, we know little.

In our thoughtless human way of living, we so often run ahead of God, making our own plans, untying the ribbons of our lives in an untimely and ungracious manner. Curiosity and impatience overcomes us, and we lose the deeper joy we might have gained. Delaying gratification is a holy task. Advent is not the dark side of Christmas but rather the place we first behold the true light of incarnation. How can our hearts know what to celebrate if we have not also questioned, waited, hoped, and suffered?

In the desert we begin to encounter God as One who tabernacles with us, even in this most difficult place. God initiates the I-Thou relationship in the wilderness, after we have walked away from Egypt's distraction and bondage. Here in the vast silences of our lives, we learn to trust, to move with God, to wait with God, to watch and listen for God's voice. Waiting for Christmas speaks of giving up a need to be in control.

When we skip waiting and circumvent the wilderness, we shortchange celebrating. The peace of Christmas will dwell with us as we wait for Christ's coming. Waiting for the coming Christ is, indeed, the precursor of Christmas. In preparation, we must set aside our wild curiosity, our need to know, our frenetic focus on selfish short-term goals. Those who would receive the true gift of Christmas must find a quiet, lonely place, a barn, a stall, a shepherd's hillside—and wait.

# Stories
# of
# Self

### BURNING BUSH REDUX

Burned with fire
but not consumed
martyrs spike horizon
rosen peaks of flame
burned with fire
and unconsumed by pain.
What mystery glows
in falling embers?
Of what significance is
sacrifice and smoke?
Holy ground, church aflame.
The burning bush is
martyrs claim.
Burned with fire
and unconsumed by pain.

# *The Lord Almighty Is* with *You*

"THE JAWS ARE HERE, we'll be able to get you out now." A voice was pulling me to the edge of consciousness.

Crunched metal and chunks of shattered safety glass hung at crazy angles from the place the windshield had been only seconds before. Like the sounds in a sick nightmare, I heard my children's voices—strange half-cries and unearthly moaning—fading, growing louder, then fading again.

The jaws? The Jaws of Life. I suddenly realized this wasn't a dream. Hours later I would learn that while on our way home from church, a pickup truck barreled through a stop sign at an intersection and hit our car broadside, wrapping it around the nearest telephone pole.

As I wandered in and out of consciousness, I felt myself being unbuckled, then lifted, and strapped securely to a board. One of my high heels was dangling from the toe of my foot and, half embarrassed, I recognized someone was removing it. The medics were discussing whether they should cut off my coat. The screaming siren tore through me, and the ambulance took the curves speeding toward the hospital. But I felt no pain—and no fear. Shock is a blessing.

At times before the accident, I found myself thinking how swiftly tragedy could invade people's lives. They go along, day in and day out, until suddenly—without warning—they are struck down by a life-changing calamity.

Secretly I wondered how I would respond to a severe crisis. My life was relatively untouched by misfortune, and I suspected it would be impossible for me to be an invalid—too impatient, always busy. Furthermore, what about my spiritual resources? Would they be adequate for a great trial? Would I keep the faith? And would my friends stick with me through difficult times? I thought of myself as the one to give to others. Would others be there for me even if I had nothing to give?

Now an accident had happened.

The second time I came to, it was in the emergency room. Our pastor was bending over me, reassuring me.

"Joanne, we love you and we're praying for you. You were in an accident, but we're so thankful that you're all alive. God is *with* you." My time in intensive care passed—a blur of muffled sounds and strange sights, interrupted from time to time by the familiar voices and the grief-stricken faces of my parents and close friends. I stared in disbelief at the tubes and monitors overhead and beside me. I was being given oxygen and a blood transfusion.

Our son, Jeremy, was wheeled in, and his bed was parked beside mine. Our eyes met. Drifting in and out of consciousness, I heard him crying and begging for water, but I couldn't help.

My mother fed me some liquids from a dinner tray, but I threw up, and the nurses were there changing my gown. When they took hold on each side of my sheet to move me, every bone and muscle in my body cried out in agony. In the next hours, nurses came several times to turn me by propping a thin pillow under my right side. The pain was excruciating.

Where are Ralph and Laura? Why don't they tell me about them? Now the fear began: maybe they weren't telling me everything. Maybe they were dead. A nurse reassured me that they had been taken to another hospital and that she would try to find out for me. Could I believe her?

Sometime later I awakened and Ralph was standing beside me, holding Laura. They both looked pitiful, with stitches and bandages all over their faces. I had seen my reflection in the gleaming metal fixtures above me and knew my face looked awful too. It didn't matter. What a relief to see them! I was too weak to move much more than my head, and my right arm was taped snugly against my body across the top of my rib cage. My right leg felt as heavy as lead. I knew I had been injured terribly and was beginning to wonder how bad it really was.

"Will I ever be able to walk again?" I searched Ralph's face for an answer that would make so much difference to my future. He'd be honest with me, and if the news was bad, he was the one to tell it.

"Dr. Watkins says it's going to be a long haul for you, but you're injuries aren't permanent. You'll be able to walk," he reassured me.

The next time I awakened, no one was nearby. A huge clock on the opposite wall read three o'clock. Large block letters on a black-and-white calendar proclaimed, "Today is Monday, January 14." In the next hours I felt the presence of God in a way I had never experienced before. Calmly I repeated the twenty-third Psalm in my mind. "Yea, though I walk through the valley of the shadow of death, I will fear no evil: for thou art with me; thy rod and thy staff they comfort me. . . ."

"God, I know this isn't an appropriate Scripture for now. This is what they say at funerals . . ."

In vain I tried to recall some other Scripture. None would come. "It's the only thing I can think of right now. . . . God, I know you're here with me. Thank-you. . . . I love you. . . ."

It seemed as if something happened in those moments that gave me strength to face the following weeks with an attitude of complete peace and calmness. On Tuesday they moved my bed down near the door of the intensive care unit. The hospital chaplain came by and handed me three envelopes which had already been opened. Surprised and grateful, I marveled at how quickly my friends must have mailed these cards.

"Perhaps you'll be strengthened in all your weakness and pain in the knowledge that ever so many people care and are praying for you. We pray that the Lord will give you enough strength to bear it, and with each strengthening God will heal you. The Lord Almighty is *with* you." I clung to the words my friend had written on an ordinary postcard.

The busy world of which I had been so much a part went on without me. Now I had only one purpose in life: to lie in bed and wait for five fractures and countless cuts and bruises to heal. The cards and letters and gifts poured in, assuring me I was abundantly blessed with friends. There was a steady stream of visitors in and out of my room.

I sent notes to Jeremy, in traction in the pediatrics unit. He also had five fractures plus cuts and bruises. "Jeremy, we don't know why this happened, but it did. It isn't an easy thing to go through, but we have to accept this accident as part of our life and try to have a good attitude. Look for the interesting things around you—talk to your visitors and nurses, and try to be cheerful and cooperative."

After ten days in bed, I was allowed to get up and stand on my left leg. My right leg couldn't bear weight because of two pelvic fractures, and my arm and shoulder were harnessed in a clavicular strap. A student nurse ran for the smelling salts when my good leg crumpled beneath me. The room was spinning as they tucked me back into bed.

Despite my first failed attempt, I desperately wanted to get to the shower. It was quite an ordeal. There I stood on one leg, positioning myself on the metal chair in the shower stall, steadying myself with my left arm. Afterward I maneuvered my useless right side back into a wheelchair. I thought then of all the handicapped people who battle their way through a lifetime of showers, clothing changes, and so many everyday activities most of us take for granted.

Later, similar thoughts came to mind when I went shopping in a wheelchair or walked into restaurants leaning on a cane. In the past I had pitied handicapped people; now *I* was handicapped, and I didn't want pity. The stares seemed to say, "Look at that poor woman. She's too young to be using a cane. What a pity she limps like that."

"Hey!" I wanted to shout at the starers, "I'm okay. I

got hurt, but I'm making it. You know . . . it could happen to you someday, too. So don't stare too hard!"

By the third week after the accident, I was back home, having been warned not to lift anything heavier than a coffee cup. After eight weeks in the hospital, Jeremy came home wearing a brace on his leg. In a few weeks, he was speeding around on his crutches, and finally with a sigh of relief, we retired the brace, the crutches, and all the other hospital junk to the attic.

We went to Florida for Easter vacation, swam, rode bicycle, and took walks on the beach. My body constantly reminded me of the wreck, but still—I was rejoicing to be alive, to be moving, to have survived!

The hair that had been shaved from my temple had grown a half inch when a piece of glass the size of a small diamond worked its way out of my scalp. The photos taken by the highway patrol arrived in the mail. We studied them off and on through the winter and into the spring. They were gruesome, and yet we wanted to look at them. Sometimes on the front page of the newspaper we'd see a similar picture—only this time someone had been killed. By the end of that year, twenty-seven people in our county had died in highway accidents. Some had survived with permanent, life-changing injury. How had I survived unharmed while others died or had their lives permanently altered?

Emma, an elderly woman from my home church, sent a beautiful six-page letter, one of over four hundred cards and letters we received. On ornate pink stationery, she wrote: "Perhaps you think it is somewhat elaborate and different . . . , perhaps the paper is more catching than the writing, but I am glad that our Lord has spared your life for a special reason. May you seek God's will in everything you do, for the Lord could have snatched your life at the turn of a hand but saw fit a purpose in your life [for you] to remain here."

I heard it so often—that God spared our lives. If God "spared" us, does God "take" others? Why did I get to walk on the beach at Easter time while another went to a rehabilitation center? Why did a friend's son die in a car crash while our son lived? The mound of a new grave in the church cemetery reminds me of how close death came. At an intersection I catch my breath, wondering and knowing it could happen again. Life is so unpredictable.

Is what happened God's providence, a miracle, or just an accident? The conviction I carried away from the twisted metal and shattered glass was not primarily a theology about suffering. I did not see the preservation of my life and the healing of my body as a sign of a special claim of God upon my life.

Yes, I asked all the questions, too, but they seemed to work themselves out quickly. Perhaps I *have* found special purpose in my life since the accident, but I have not endeavored, in any way, to "pay God back."

Understanding about the meaning of the accident in my life came when I returned in my mind—as I do many times—to the indescribable inner peace which permeated my body and soul as I lay in the intensive care unit after the accident. God was present in my greatest crisis, in my hour of deepest need. It has been easier to trust, easier to believe in a future, ever since the Lord Almighty walked with me to the edge of the valley of the shadow.

# *Vocation*

### ADVICE TO MY WRITING TEACHER

Speak to me of imagery,
style, tone, and diction,
of line and song,
of hymn and fiction.
Talk to me of plot
and characterization.
Give me your tools,
poetic rules,
suggest compression,
personification,
assign alliteration.
Find ways to stimulate,
invite me to create,
tempt my imagination.
Do all the things you do
and do so well.
Only, take care,
hold back,
go gently with my words:
I'm still a fragile poet.
Dwell softly on a hint
of pure expression;
sift lightly through my pain
and true confession;
and don't critique
unveiled revelation.

# How I Became a Writer

PERHAPS THE FAVORITE story of any writer is the one that tells "How I Became a Writer." It is my best story because in the telling one renews a special bond uniting all who share the pain and passion for writing—the blessed burden.

In the beloved *Charlotte's Web*, a literary classic disguised as a children's story, author E. B. White ends with these startling words: "It is not often that someone comes along who is a true friend and a good writer. Charlotte was both." Perhaps when White penned those words, he was thinking of his friend, James Thurber, at *The New Yorker*. I think of Katie—but I'm getting ahead of my story.

I became a writer in the middle of the night in a hotel in Columbus. It was at a Christian women's retreat where a well-known author was the keynote speaker; I was thirty years old—and restless. At the conference book stand one afternoon, a new book by our speaker caught my attention. Inside was a chapter titled, "On Turning Thirty." It was amazing! This woman knew me—she *was* me! A few pages back was another chapter: "I Want To Write." Here were words I'd never dared to say, even to myself. With this sudden recognition came unexpected tears.

All night I lay awake reviewing my life. God, in that

Jacob-wrestling-with-the-angel experience, was calling. It seems absurd to me now—my excuse was lame: I couldn't type.

God didn't care. And I emerged the next morning marked for life, a writer.

At an autographing session that day, I carefully opened my new purchase to the first page of the "I Want To Write" chapter. A chat with the author, her inscription on that particular page, would seal my vow and launch my career. Scarcely glancing at me, she flipped the pages to the inside cover and wrote her standard inscription. Disappointed, but shy, I only said "Thank you."

In response to my letter, sent the following week, she mailed a mimeographed page of tips for beginning writers and put me on the mailing list of her religious radio broadcast. I was disappointed.

I sat up nights and wrote my first book, had someone type it, and sent it off. Rejection letters dribbled in. I attended a writers' workshop. I read books about writing. I wrote. I read. I became a stringer for the local newspaper. I learned to type.

One afternoon, while reading our denominational magazine, Katie Funk Wiebe's essay caught my attention. Here was someone else to admire: a seasoned author from my own church tradition. In those days there were not so many women writers in our church. Katie's writing was thought-provoking, and at the same time, it touched the senses.

This piece was about hunger and human need and chocolate pie. "This, God! Oh please, God, this!" I prayed. "Let me write like this!" Tears again. And then . . . determination to meet Katie. Here was one who could feed my hunger—a hunger that had nothing to do with chocolate pie and everything to do with my longing to become a writer.

My dream came true when a committee at our school invited Katie Funk Wiebe to present a guest lecture. She flew in from Kansas, and I met her at the airport. She was petite with a white cap of hair, cut in a becoming style. Her voice was a pleasant mixture of Kansas and Canada. She was brisk and crisp and warm all at the same time.

In my nervous excitement, I forgot to offer to stop and buy her dinner, and we missed a turn and took the long way home. However, by the next afternoon, she had read some of my writing (carefully displayed on my kitchen bulletin board for her benefit), and we were drinking tea and talking like college roommates.

Katie coached me in my first real steps as a writer, for by now I had learned that becoming a writer is more a process than a declaration. "Attend writers' workshops," Katie counseled me. "Read *Christianity Today* and *Christian Century* to get balance and perspective on Christian issues. Write and rewrite. Don't give up. Write letters and opinion pieces for the newspaper and church newsletter. Put a desk in the corner of your kitchen and keep writing. You can do it."

Katie told me to call myself a writer. It is not enough to simply dabble in writing as a hobby, to think of it as a side road of one's life. Writing is a vocation, a calling, the definition of who one is as a person—like Jo in *Little Women*. A true writer will never successfully quit writing, although she may try. Katie said she herself had quit at least twice.

To be sure, there were others who guided me on my way: the genial area-desk editor at our small-town newspaper; the editor of a Sunday school paper who gave me a chance to rewrite when my work didn't suit him; instructors at writers' workshops. Still, Katie was special. She took an interest in me that went far beyond grammar and punctuation—in fact, we rarely spoke of such things.

Over the next two years, I followed Katie around to various retreats and conferences. One wonderful week I devoured her wisdom and expert guidance at a Christian writers' conference. We sat together at mealtimes and talked of many things. At the end of that week, with undiluted delight and pride, I accepted first prize in nonfiction writing. My friend was ecstatic and took me out for a hot fudge sundae to celebrate.

Katie has a way of confiding in me that builds our friendship. When she writes to me, she usually tells me about her writing projects, including some of her struggles and frustrations. When we meet periodically at church conferences and the like, she'll pull me aside, invite me into her room, and offer me a granola bar from her suitcase. She instructs me in the things she has learned about travel and public speaking and making one's way in church circles.

I shall always treasure a special conversation at General Assembly. We happened to be together when we met Paul M. Schrock, head of the book division at Herald Press. Katie introduced us, and the three of us chatted about the new books and trends in book publishing. There in that intimate inner circle, talking to one of Katie's mentors, I realized that Herald Press would take my submission seriously—because of Katie.

Occasionally now, someone will tell me that my writing reminds them of the writing of Katie Funk Wiebe. "Has anyone ever told you that?" they ask. Little do they know how much their question means to me. For I've come to believe that in some strange way it's true.

Last week Katie wrote me another letter. She had just read something I wrote. "You're really developing into an excellent writer," she told me. "Keep up the good work!"

I will.

Surely, it is a potential embarrassment to keep company with a would-be writer. I marvel at the energy it took for a college professor, with abundant writing projects of her own, not to mention a family, to find time to write letters and keep up a friendship with someone who took three decades just to say "I want to write!"

It's almost difficult to recall the young woman who tossed and turned all night worrying about typing. Today, if I wanted a famous author to inscribe my book in an unconventional way, I would step up and tell her so. Self-confidence and courage are by-products of my new life as a writer.

And writing has a wonderful way of helping me pin down the stray ideas that used to float helplessly by in the fog. Writing and thinking fit together in my life and create a wholeness impossible for me in any other way.

I keep a folder of letters written by a writer, to a writer. They are a memoir of one who has learned firsthand the truth: It is not often that someone comes along who is a true friend and a good writer, but for some who are especially blessed, it really only has to happen once.

# *Roles*

### INNER SANCTUM

The kitchen table
checkered cloth
cookies baked
oven's off.
Dripping faucet
humming fridge
tea is steeping
lift the lid.
Mugs are hanging
on the wall.
Sip the tea
till it is all.
Think your thoughts
dream your dreams
a kitchen's more
than it sometimes seems.

# Three Faces of Joanne

FEW PEOPLE KNOW I am mad. I manage to appear normal. But "wholeness," such a popular term these days, is foreign to me. My madness is manifest in small ways, invisible to the untrained eye. A literature book lies on my kitchen counter. The receptionist at my office forwards a call from my ten-year-old. There are grocery coupons and class notes in my tote. Perhaps to you this is evidence of mere disorganization. I assure you it is, rather, a multiple-personality disorder.

Karen Mains, a woman who struggled as I struggle, once wrote, "The artist denied is often neurotic." When I turned thirty, I finally grasped the truth of this statement in my own case and set out to avoid neurosis. I chose to become a writer—a poet and an artist—and that choice precipitated my present madness. You will soon see what I mean, for in the urgency to avoid neurosis, I unwittingly stumbled into a life that sometimes seems impossible to live. I am mad. And I survive by drinking.

So you ask, "What makes you mad?" and "Who are you really, Joanne?" The answer all depends on what I'm drinking at the moment.

In the morning and most of every evening, I'm my Domestic Self. Time was, this was *all* I was, Domestic Self. That was it. My Domestic Self brews tea. A teakettle whistles and the domestic person answers. Tea is what you drink while you're clipping coupons and writing grocery lists. You give it to a child whose stomach is off. You serve fancy teas in pretty teacups from a pretty teapot at your temporarily lace-draped kitchen table.

You push aside the teacups on the table and fold laundry or talk over a problem with your teenager. You ice the tea in summer and give it to a tired husband at the end of a long day when you didn't get dinner started on time. (With some luck he may offer to grill something.)

It is the Domestic Self that feels the first stirring of life. The self that indulges the nesting urge and makes curtains for the kitchen window. The Domestic Self—this tea person—knows the longing to frame a simple concise view of the world from her kitchen sink.

The tea life is relatively simple. Oh, there is the matter of cream and sugar and trays and silver tea services and cookies and sandwiches, but on the whole you know what's expected. You do what needs doing. The Domestic Self is easy to be when that's the only self you are. It gets harder when it has to fit with other selves.

My Career Woman Self drinks coffee. I have a very warm relationship with coffee. A coffee career woman will probably have a commuter cup filled with coffee beside her in the car. Coffee is the first smell that greets you when you enter the office. The coffeepot is the hub of the building.

The coffee career woman looks forward to coffee breaks. At my office, where I write news, edit other people's attempts at writing, and in general keep my eyes glued to a computer screen for large blocks of time, it's a relief to share a cup of coffee with a co-worker, to look into someone's eyes, to pour my troubles into another's cup.

When you share coffee at the office, you share the earthy aroma of a life of hard work. An earthenware coffee mug will find its way onto your desk. Next thing you know, it will be filled with pens and pencils and scissors and an X-acto knife. Coffee gets spilled on the staff meeting minutes, and no one really cares. It's understood. The boss never says anything about drinking coffee at your desk. He drinks at his desk too.

A lot is expected of the coffee career person. She is expected to know how to enter and exit a file on the computer and to back up her data every day. She is expected to meet deadlines, write reports, give reports, read and follow memos, sort mail, send mail, make assignments, follow up on assignments, and think ahead to next month's agenda. She is expected to pay attention to the budget, attend staff meetings, and provide input when asked.

Coffee is the comfort that gets you through a day of work. It's fun to be a coffee career person. You get to have your own desk. If you're lucky, as I am, you even have your own room. It feels good to know you're "out there." At the office you look at life through slatted mini-blinds. You learn to adjust, to see through the slats, to read between the lines. When you're a career woman, coffee gets you through.

The coffee career life is difficult, but not impossible to master. If you start out in an office that isn't too demanding and have the tea life down fairly well beforehand, you can switch from coffee to tea at a moment's notice. It becomes almost automatic. You hook your finger in the cup and sip. Instantly you know where you are. You find your place and make your way. Life is varied and interesting, and there are always new things to see through the miniblinded window.

It was the wine that got me into trouble. In my particular case, the wine came before the coffee and after the tea. (In point of fact, I don't actually drink real wine anymore. I do drink coffee and tea. I quit drinking even my one or two yearly celebrative glasses of wine after a friend's son was killed by a drunken driver.)

Soon after I decided to become a writer, so as not to be neurotic, I began to long for instruction in becoming a writer. Books about writing were not enough, so I took a class. One thing led to another, and I ended up in college majoring in communications. I wanted my writing to count for something, which is to say, I wanted people to read what I wrote.

College for me was like wine. Almost too stimulating. I had to take it in small doses, and even then I would come home drunken with some new idea or inebriated from the sound of a certain combination of words I discovered in my English literature text. I stumbled on new ideas at every turn of the page. The teachers were fountains spewing forth. I discovered how thirsty I was. Some new window was open, and my Wine-of-Learning Self caught the fresh breezes and breathed in deeply.

It wasn't easy, switching from wine to tea and back again on an almost daily basis, but I managed. I discovered that if I tried, I could nearly keep the domestic-tea life separate from the wine-of-learning life. Once in awhile I would forget and launch into some discussion of Dante's *Inferno* at the supper table, or I'd find myself thinking about a communication theory when my hands were in the dishwater. After supper I'd sometimes browse through *Arts and Ideas* instead of the grocery ads. But on the whole, the parallel lives were manageable, and I got along.

Unfortunately, in my case this stage was relatively short because I was offered a wonderful part-time job in —of all things—communications. How could I turn down an opportunity to write and be read? But how could I quit indulging my newly acquired thirst for the wine of learning? Tea, coffee, wine, I opted to have it all, and sometimes it's almost too much. I am mad, but I am not neurotic.

I cope with life by sipping slowly whatever cup I'm holding at a particular moment. Solitude is mandatory. Silence is sacred. In the busy days, I hold on, believing someday everything will come together. There is coffee in the faculty lounge. The ten-year-old will go to college. People will read my writing; they already are. But just now this is my cup. And I drink it with joy.

## CREATIVITY

Before
  pencil
    touches paper
the mind
  begins
its
  free fall
into
  inner space
    where
it
  grasps
    at
wisps
  of
    life
  not
easily
  caught
    or
      held.

# Free Fall into Inner Space

ALREADY ON THE FIRST DAY of second semester, I surmised I would be thinking much about creativity—on second thought—spell that with a capital *C* and add an exclamation point: Creativity! In their first lectures, both the creative writing professor and the graphic communications instructor emphasized the importance they place on strengthening the students' creative thinking skills. "I'm not here to teach you how to write. I'm here to help you teach yourself to write," said Mrs. Rodak.

"See that corner over there?" said Mrs. Drennan, pointing to a corner in the art lab. "When you are backed into a corner, and you think there is no place to go, just remember that there are twenty solutions to every problem. . . ." She proceeded to have us describe possible ways to get out of that corner. That's the beauty of art. It helps us look at things in new ways, see the possibilities in life's corners.

Next thing I knew, both instructors were trying to engage me in "creativity exercises." Drawing eight different sketches of the same insect was scarier for me than writing a poem. The art teacher told us to "do something" with a page full of circles; that wasn't quite as threatening. I was amused, though, with the goofy-looking ladybugs I produced; one carried a polka-dot umbrella. The lightning bug held a lantern, and the doodlebug's spots swirled everywhere. In my estimation, they weren't very good, but I was surprised I could do the assignment at all; at first I'd been sure I couldn't. By the end of the semester, my artistic confidence had increased a bit. That had been the whole point of the exercises.

From the art lab, I'd trek across the campus to see what activity the writing teacher would bring to class. Her exercises were designed to stimulate, and I promptly rebelled. It made me angry when she showed us a video of forests, cascading streams, and ferns, and then asked us to write a poem. In a fit of dissension, I wrote out my angry feelings, and Eureka! I had coalesced. (Mrs. Rodak later used my piece as an example when *she* wrote an article about teaching creative writing.)

I'd thought of myself as a creative person from the time I was young, but I had never judged creativity a thing to cultivate, to nurse along. "This class is painful for me," one student confided after class. I'm not sure what *she* meant, but I was dealing with a superior attitude I'd adopted during one of those first sessions.

After a few classes, I began to realize that in the past I had always missed the point of creativity exercises. We all need help breaking out of what Thorstein Veblen calls "trained incapacities." We are educated until we believe in what we *can't* do: we narrow ourselves to those things we think we can do. We believe there is a right way to do most things. We become more and more sure of our limitations in drawing a bug—even one kind, let alone eight! We are stuck in a corner and can't crawl out. We never consider flying.

We need a paradigm shift in our thinking. The word *paradigm* has almost become a buzzword in corporate circles because of a popular video circulating in the executive world. It is called *The Business of Paradigms,* by Joel Arthur Barker. Paradoxically, it uses the uninspired format of a talking head to explain how businesses and individuals limit their creative potential. A paradigm is a pattern, a macro, a cliché—the way we've always done it. When we consider those things we've always believed—for instance, that a bicycle seat must be a fixed saddle, or that a watch must have a mainspring —we automatically rule out other ways of creating a product. The Swiss rejected the quartz digital watch because it seemed contrary to the way watches had always been made. Texas Instruments saw the possibilities. So far, to my discomfort, most bicycle seats are still made using the horse saddle paradigm!

After I broke the paradigm in my own mind about how creativity appears—that it is some natural gift I was born with—I began to understand that it works much the same for everyone. There are many ways to nurture and enhance creativity.

By learning to cultivate my creativity, I am learning "how to feed and keep a Muse," as the prolific writer Ray Bradbury advises. I am more consciously implementing the suggestions I received in creative writing class. Keeping a journal where I can experiment with words and phrases and new forms is not so much a discipline as a natural expression of who I am, a nurturer of solitude. In the past, I had never connected physical and mental energy, but now I discover that my best creations appear after a walk or some physical activity. Rest and relaxation restore my spirit and allow me to find life's poetry.

I am still discovering the value of visualization—using my inner eye to recreate scenes from the past. This skill is connected to another requisite, enhancing the powers of observation. Yes, the weeds along the road are beautiful, but exactly how purple is the flower on the thistle? Later I shall find words; for now, I will feast my eyes on the sumptuous blossom. I choose to absorb *just this* vision of the rose bush in my neighbor's garden right down to that lonely, lingering bud of mid-October which waits for imminent frost. Sometime, perhaps, these visions of weeds and roses will somehow express my own Thoreau-like "yearning for wildness."

Meanwhile, I delight in life's variety, give myself permission to try new things, meet new people, or make new observations about people I already know; these all nourish the creative impulse. I intentionally foster interests and curiosity: journalism started me in observing life. With the arts I encounter new channels. Watching a play or movie often feeds the Muse and sets me off in new directions. Vacations in a different part of the country, viewing palm trees or rocky terrain, open my mind. A hike, a tour of a neighboring village, practicing concentration as I observe the details of a home I am visiting for the first time—all might allow something different to happen in my mind at some later time. Who knows?

Encouraging this inner solitude activates my imagination and suggests a world of endless possibilities. Unfortunately, in our business, instead of looking for potentiality, many people live their lives in a comfortable series of clichés. In computer language, everyday life becomes a macro. A macro is a byte of information programmed into the computer so that it can be retrieved with the stroke of one key. It's handy to have my name, address, phone number, and social security number available at the stroke of the *J* key, for instance. But pulling up a series of macros would never produce a poem.

More and more now, I approach my writing as other artists approach their art: with an attitude of experimentation and exploration. I can never be sure what will come out but do not hesitate to rearrange it, destroy parts of it, add other discoveries to it. With abandon I reshape what comes. Insert, delete, block, and move—these are my favorite computer keys!

Explaining all of this somehow deadens what takes place when things come together and suddenly I am flying, floating. It is not a matter of performing some prescribed set of tasks as outlined above and then settling down doggedly to produce prose. I am learning that the exercise of creativity requires a measure of solitude, relaxation, reflection, and most of all, trust. A belief that something will happen when I sit down to write. More and more often things do happen. Trust builds.

Yet before the trust there is often a time of frustration, confusion, and disruption—a period of madness, when one feels incapable of managing any part of life, let alone producing a work of art. Then finally, or suddenly, and often unexpectedly, the mind begins its free fall into inner space where it grasps at wisps of life at first not easily caught or held. Then I wonder why it was so hard; why I didn't trust more. I am exhilarated—in some other world, where I hang on and gloat, obsessed with my creation, yet never sure just where these foreign words came from or how they appeared, just so, in just this arrangement on the page.

But my Muse will not be entrapped or held. No, only enticed to return again when conditions are all finally exactly right once more. With practice and diligence, the mysterious, graceful Muse might return more often and stay longer. That's what I'm hoping. I bumble along, celebrating the mystery and the grace of something called "Creativity!" Somehow I was able in one moment, perhaps then another and another, to let go of old ways, old thoughts, old habits, old ideas, old words. It is an epiphany of grace, and I obsessively cling to it.

"Let yourself be disrupted. Confusion is grace. . . ." The words of a Salvadoran priest come to me at just the moment I am thinking about creativity, and the two are mysteriously linked in my mind. I am teaching myself to write. Metaphors mutate, and my mind, aided at times by a thesaurus, substitutes sparkling words for tarnished ones. I am flying, free-falling, fleeing my corner. Beyond that, I can't explain it.

*Fear*

## ASH WEDNESDAY

Father wakes me
stirring up the coal
in the cellar furnace
fanning into flame
the gift of another day,
kindling a fire of love
in the family circle
with blackened scoop shovel
and crooked rusty poker.
I hear love in ashes
carried out by the bucketful
where they write on snow
of duty and compassion
largely filled.

But a monster woman lives
under the cold air return.
The angular grid
at the bottom of the stairs
her talons cutting bare feet.
Grooches' growl echoes back
when she's hollered at,
her face a dusty oval
peering up through
the icy grate defies me
to face danger, fight fear,
laugh at evil, pursue good.

After oatmeal sisters
huddle in the living room
beside the hot-air register
soaking up warm,
melting peeled crayons
on shiny waffle.
Down the rusted chute
new colors stream
uncharted into the
bowels of the house
blazing fiery glory
on the coldest morning
of winter.

# *If It's Something Serious*

A WHITE-HOT POKER of fear pierces my body some-where to the right of the place where, moments ago, I found "the lump"—a round, smooth, dreadful thing.

Now my fingers probe the firm knot beneath the soft outer layer of tissue while my thoughts race from "lump," to "cancer," to "radical surgery," to "death." Somehow all four words become a tangled mass of thought, a mental tumor that consumes the mind. When I try to rank them in order of horror, I cannot.

It is a long, torturous night. The rhythmic whir of the fan stirs the stale air of the bedroom. I toss and turn and check "the lump." Outside, the foolish little cicadas chirp away in their endless conversations that don't inter-est me. I am thinking of Barbara and Orpha and other women who began and finally ended long, painful jour-neys that started with "a lump."

I am awakened from fitful sleep by the seven o'clock church chimes. On other days the chimes serve as a kind of religious alarm clock; I listen through the "bongs" to sing along with the hymn. This morning the "bongs" echo Donne: "Never send to know for whom the bell tolls; / it tolls for thee."

Fully awake now, I recall my dream of wrecked cars—a flashback from our serious accident, years ago. In the dream I was in a blue sedan that smashed head-on into a tree. A red truck rammed it from behind, and the roof split open.

At times like this, one is especially glad for a good doctor, not only a competent one—there are plenty of those around—but a *good* one. I chose Dr. Hutson some time ago because I think his manner is right.

A doctor should be professional and not paternalistic. He (or she) should be friendly, but not boisterous, exuberant, or overly impressed with himself. He should notice your questions and give you concise answers that are informative but not include more detail than you care to know. Above all, he should at least strive to give you the illusion that he has plenty of time for you.

I never quite get used to disrobing for a male doctor. Lying exposed and vulnerable on the hard examination table, I used to stare at the ceiling tile and pretend I wasn't there. This time, Dr. Hutson informs me ahead of time what the exam will include, and I am forced by his questions to participate.

My gown is a crisp, floral print, open down the back. I alternately slip each arm out of the sleeve and allow the doctor to examine me while answering his questions: Did I breast-feed my babies? Did I notice any discharge? Do I do regular self-examinations? When did I first notice the lump? Have I had any lumps before?

The doctor is concerned. He carefully fastens the single loop at the back of the gown. Then he reassures me that a lump is something to check out, but we are not wise to jump to premature conclusions about it. Still, he's not taking chances. He's working fast. I am to have a mammogram at the hospital tomorrow morning and then see the doctor who reads the X-rays. He might do a needle biopsy. He is a surgeon.

I ask questions about this doctor's philosophy of treatment for breast cancer—although, thinking about it later, I'm not sure either Dr. Hutson or I used the word "cancer." We most certainly didn't talk about "radical mastectomy" and, of course, the word "death" is hardly even in the vocabulary of anyone anymore.

My card at the hospital is terribly out of date. A flip young woman creates a computer file on me. Her too-long fingernails, splashed with glittered, coral-color, chipped polish, scarcely fit on the keys. She is wearing an inappropriate black chiffon sheath, and I feel sorry for her and forgive her abrupt manner, which signals that this is her first job and that she's insecure.

Down the hall, the X-ray technician stands in contrast to Miss Fingernails. Her smooth blond bob is fitting for someone in a white uniform. She asks a few questions and gives a gracious in-depth explanation of the procedure. She emphasizes the fact that she may do a repeat X-ray, but that should not alarm me, since it's standard procedure.

The room is decorated in predictable pink, with velvet-covered French provincial chairs and the obligatory impressionistic print of a young girl in a flowing dress and hat. Once again I am given a gown, pink this time.

The examination by the doctor is routine compared to the mammography. There is no experience so lacking in dignity as that of standing in front of a monstrous machine with a portion of your anatomy on a frigid glass shelf where it is squeezed and flattened by a vise, and then photographed. The gown is entirely useless, hanging from one shoulder.

I am reminded of the time I observed the taping of an informative television show about breast cancer. On camera, the speaker told the female talk-show host that having mammography was simple and painless. After the taping, she confided to the interviewer, "Really, it hurts like hell!"

She was right, although I would not have used the same language.

I am released from the machine and from the ban on deodorant (which contains aluminum) and coffee. Coffee is thought to cause fibrocystic breast disease and is prohibited a month before one has a mammogram because cysts could distort it. In the perverse reasoning of the medical community, I was required to abstain for only eight hours.

I drive to McDonalds for a large coffee. In front of me, on the way, is a truck hauling a pink marble headstone with the name "Barth" on it.

From the tangled mass of thought, a new idea forms: "It could be a cyst."

My first irrational fear is replaced by a benign thought that resembles hope but at this stage is still probably closer to a wish.

"It's no use worrying," I tell myself. "You don't even know what it is."

As for what it *could* be, I try to remember that, if it should be "something serious," I'll have time to get used to it. At least more than one night.

"You would get used to things gradually if it was 'something serious.' You can get used to a lot of things when you do it gradually," I remind myself.

While sipping the cup of comforting hot coffee, I come to a conclusion about what's important: if "the lump" turns out to mean "surgery," "cancer," or even "death," I still have hope!

# *Maturity*

## FLEDGED

The nest is too small
and you are grown
out of us
young and bold
flying free
in some other
constellation.

How could you know
I still imagine
the music of
your presence
wishing you back
to fill the kitchen
and empty my refrigerator.

# *You Never Forget How to Skate*

IT WAS FREDDIE AMSTUTZ,* I think, who wrote the ditty that said, "I could have danced all night, but I'm a Mennonite, and we don't think it's right. . . . I would have found it so delightful, but the bishop thought it frightful."

We glided around the bishop's prohibition gracefully—on skates. My dad made it easy for us by building a farm pond at the expense of the government, which happened to be promoting a water-conservation project at the time.

One cold, blustery night while my mother was at Mary-Martha Fellowship, Dad took us to a secondhand store and purchased ice skates for everyone, including himself.

After that, cold weather took on a whole new meaning. When John Reese offered to lace up my skates, I thought I'd died and gone to heaven. And when I saw how well Mervin Landes couple-skated, I even reconsidered the original "hayseed" judgment I'd bestowed on him. (Being near him was tolerable if I wrapped a muffler over my nose to block out the smell of his barn clothes.)

Roller-skating came some time later. I discovered that one who knows how to ice-skate can easily learn roller skating. But, for me, ice skates have always seemed less clumsy; and it's easier to stop. Still, roller-skating made the whole moving-with-a-member-of-the-opposite-sex more appealing. At the roller rink, when they announced a couple-skate, everyone knew what was expected; on the ice, however, things sometimes were pretty vague. Besides, at the Rollerarena, we could skate to music.

I recall all of this years later—in my mid-thirties with two kids in the back seat and a good-looking husband beside me. We are desperate for meaningful family activity. "You'll see," I counsel glibly. "You never forget how to skate."

Is Skate World smaller than the Rollerarena, or is it just that I'm grown-up now? I am soon reassured. Some things never change: the revolving lights, the many-faceted silver ball suspended from the ceiling, the rows of benches behind a carpeted barricade, the gorgeous couple waltzing with liquid grace, the two thin men with whistles around their necks who skate effortlessly, and mostly backward.

The rental skates still have dents in the toes. We put our feet in them and feel the crumbling insole. I wriggle my toes and wonder how many germs can work their way through the fibers of my too-thin socks. Do they ever replace the laces? The laces on my skates are frayed about an inch or more on each end, although one is tied into a rather slim knot that still fits through the eyelets. After lacing my seven-year-old daughter's skates, I resolutely begin on my own, stuffing the frayed end into one eyelet after another. The ticket woman, a nice lady with dyed hair and red fingernails, sees my trouble and brings clamps for the ends of the laces. She solders them with her cigarette lighter.

I'm ready to roll. Or am I? Weaving out onto the

floor, I suddenly realize who I am: a middle-aged mother whose kids persuaded her to go roller-skating. The mirror at the end of the rink doesn't lie. I'm uptight, uncoordinated and . . . older. Other skaters casually whiz by, snapping their fingers to the beat, crossing the right leg confidently over the left at the curve, toeing to a stop just short of the barricade.

I crash uninhibitedly into the padded half-wall, and my son whips around me, a picture of confidence. Spent, I retire to the snack bar where my partner and I share a plate of nachos. "I haven't skated in sixteen years," I announce breathlessly to the girl behind the counter. She doesn't seem surprised. "I could tell," she remarks bluntly. "You ought to come at least once a week."

By the time I finish my diet Coke and we get back onto the floor, the deejay is spinning an old '60s tune. It's easier to skate to "That Old Time Rock 'n' Roll." I catch my partner's hand, and we dance the couple-skate. I think how nice it is to have a steady guy—never again to know the agony of sitting in the dim light at the end of the rink waiting for someone who doesn't even know I exist to ask me to skate. Tonight's date is a great partner, but he squeezes my hand so hard that my wedding ring makes an indentation on my pinky.

The song ends but it's still a couple-skate. My almost-teenaged son drifts up and takes my arm. We make a lovely couple, and I give him some pointers that will help him impress girls at the next skating party. In another part of my brain, I'm trying to figure out how it is that I have a son old enough to care about girls and to couple-skate. If only I could quit thinking about what my feet are doing and spend some time figuring out what happened to me since becoming a grown-up. What does it mean to be a grown-up anyway?

It's not an environment conducive to contemplation, yet I want to search out all the meaning this evening has for me. Instead, I give in and wrap up the frayed ends of my thoughts. They're playing "Girls Just Wanna Have Fun," and I decide maybe it's okay just to enjoy skating and think later. The stuffy "Mom" compartment of my brain holds out just a bit longer, reminding me that moms aren't supposed to like modern music. I ruthlessly quash conventional mother instinct.

My body relaxes and the rhythm of the music pumps me around the rink. I sail past my son and wave to my daughter wobbling on the arm of my date. My two skating partners are playing a video game when I finally ease off the floor, not even touching the barricade. I note that Skate World isn't much different from the Rollerarena in another way: video games now replace the once-forbidden pinball machines.

Thinking about this experience later, I will undoubtedly uncover additional profound meaning in tonight's exercise. For now, it seems enough to have proved that you never forget how to skate.

---

* Names have been changed to protect the innocent.

# Walking
## in
## Holiness

*Excellence*

## MAY BURIAL

The silver blade slices
damp earth, turning clods
to sun and wind
folding perfectly green
slices of life
down to death.

New earth inhales
of May perfumery
and drinks dew;
brilliant potential—
the four-inch fringe
of would-be meadow
swallowed to summer
by a plow.

Youth cut down
and folded in
breaks nature's expectation;
fragile seedlings
live to thank a silver blade
while turned-down grasses
languish in the
subterranean grave.

# In Serch of Excelence

"MY GREATEST FEAR," someone confessed to me recently, "is that I'll just be average."

"The average person *is* average," I said, trying to provide some encouragement. I have no great fear of being average—probably always knew I was except for a time when I thought I might be below average because of failed math tests.

Even though I'm average, I pride myself in being organized. I once spoke on the topic at a women's retreat and put together a list of tips to help homemakers be more organized. For the past year, I've been faithfully organizing my coupons and recently even hung all my necklaces on nails on the wall of my closet.

Every so often I go on an organization kick, sorting papers, getting rid of old clothes and magazines, cleaning out the kitchen junk drawer, and sending a dozen white elephants to the great Goodwill box in the sky. I once sewed a special cleaning apron that was supposed to make me a more organized cleaning person.

Marketers cash in on this organizational obsession. Diet clubs and aerobics classes offer special introductory fees in January when people shape up and break in fresh appointment books. Organizer gadgets sell well in January and again in September. Perhaps we hope a new set of plastic on our desks, on our garage shelves, or in our kitchens will help us achieve a status somewhere above average, well into the range of excellent, organized, and perfect.

If intellectual pursuits are my forte, I may choose to purchase one of the many excellent books that point the way to excellent living, whether that excellence be achieved in family relationships, on the job, or in regard to health or appearance.

Christians value excellence as much as those in secular society. Many of us have accepted the world's message that we must strive for excellence in all we do. Many Christians have made "self-actualization," that condition whereby we reach our full and highest potential, an important element of their life philosophy. Becoming all we were meant to be is seen as a Christian virtue. After all, doesn't the Bible say, "Whatever your hand finds to do, do it with your might?" (Eccles. 9:10).

Abraham Maslow, a widely known psychologist, introduced Maslow's hierarchy of needs, a nifty triangular chart that appears in every introductory psychology textbook. The pyramid describes categories of human need, starting with basic needs for safety and security, adding layers of social needs, esteem needs, and finally at the pinnacle, self-actualization. (One wonders how self-actualization and other "needs" of a person fit with the "needs" of family members and others. This isn't addressed in the chapter where the psychologists draw triangles.)

In a book titled *Excellence,* author John Gardner writes: "What we must reach for is a conception of perpetual self-discovery, . . . perpetual reshaping to realize one's best self, . . . to be the person one *could* be."

Another excellence writer, Ted Engstrom, writes: "If you are willing to be the person you were meant to be, . . . I think you will discover that *for you* the sky is the limit. . . . Excellence demands that you be better than yourself." (How, I ask, can I be better than myself?)

Society is marketing excellence, and I'm buying. Self-actualization has me scrambling up the mountain and fighting the battle for excellence. But in a reflective moment, one wonders if the chosen actions and mind-set might actually be selfish or an indication of an unwholesome self-interest.

Is excellence and self-actualization, as described by these writers, the key to robust Christian discipleship? Or is this self-interest evidence that the Christian community has bought too much into society's values? Is self-actualization actually selfishness? Is the excellence philosophy the way of the cross?

A cartoon depicts two workers, tools in hand, eyeing the "Great American Monument to Mediocrity." The monument is perched on a hill (Maslow's pyramid?), and one side is propped up with three bricks. "Oh, that's good enough!" quips the supervisor to the construction worker. Might it be okay to erect a monument to mediocrity and then move on to build relationships and practice humility?

Working hard to achieve a goal, striving to improve oneself, getting organized, taking opportunities—these cannot be wrong. Yet the pursuit of perfection and excellence can become a trap, preventing us from trying things we can't do perfectly or leading us to overwork and unrealistic expectations. Pursuit of perfection can also lead to the neglect of the needs of others and the

barrenness of a life with no room for the cultivation of relationships.

There are times in life when "good enough" will
do. Still, one struggles with the "good enough"-excel-
lence dichotomy. How does one guard against self-
centeredness and the root of selfishness which lurks beneath the surface of a pursuit of excellence? What happens when my pursuit conflicts with the pursuit of others
in my circle? In what sphere do I pursue this excellence—work? home? relationships? hobbies? or all of
the above? Where is the balance between my own needs,
desires, and self-actualization and that of my children,
spouse, and co-workers?

I think I should be less entangled in the pursuit of
excellence and more involved in seeking disciplined living as a disciple. There is an element of grace and humility in discipleship. A refusal to push, to climb, to achieve.
A willingness to bend and seek and wait—even to let go,
give way, give up, lay down, bow out. Perhaps to die to
self.

Even in the smallest things, God's grace drifts in
around my need. Christian literature is filled with stories
of ways God meets material need. In past weeks I heard
two people share stories about how God met a material
need in a miraculous way. A missionary, who needed
funds for a major car repair bill, received a monetary gift
of almost the same amount and was told by the giver to
use it wherever it was needed. A woman who received a
request from a needy family found a store owner willing
to donate exactly the item required.

My needs are often spiritual and emotional rather
than material. Too often I forget to come into God's pres-

ence with a need—be it material, emotional, or spiritual. Like a toddler, I am too quick to "do it myself." Would Christian excellence bid me seek, or perhaps trust and wait?

Some of my perceived needs, including a need for excellence, lead me away from the posture of one who is willing to wait, to put my own needs on hold in order to minister to the needs of another perhaps more needy. I escape "average" and "ordinary" and in flight lose sight of a God who will provide all my needs—a God who is honored by selfless living.

While it is true that Jesus commanded his disciples to be perfect—modeling God's perfection—there is no suggestion in Scripture that our perfection is self-made. It is a perfection which comes from being disciples who are God-directed, not goal-directed. Our mission is not to lead perfect lives or excellent lives or self-actualized lives. As disciples, we are to be first of all servants of God and of each other. It is a difficult calling in a world obsessed with achievement.

The words of the prophet Isaiah are echoed in an old Quaker poem and depict, for me, the life of Christian excellence. The disciple's search for excellence leads us to

Find the lost,
Heal the broken,
Feed the hungry,
Release the prisoner,
Rebuild the nations,
Bring peace among people,
And make music in the heart.

Could answering the call of God lead us, not to the pinnacle of the self-actualization and excellence pyramid, but to cross-bearing servant-living sacrifice, suffering, and humility? Or to ask the question another way: Is Mother Teresa into excellence and self-actualization?

## REBIRTH

From shadowy canal
of emergence
new life springs
    beneath
    unseen fingers
moist gray smooth clay
  answers the summons
of negative
    positive space
parading shamelessly
    into existence
    dancing a spritely
love song
    on enchanting
    fields of dream
where form defines
    clay spirits
and earth rejoices
at the good fortune
    of dust.

# The Cadence of Friendship

HOW THE FOUR OF US CAME to be pedaling bicycles in the rain up what our tour leaders called "rolling hills" of Vermont is a long story. We weren't thinking much about it while rivulets of water were cascading over our fluorescent yellow helmets and dripping off onto our noses.

I now have a whole volume of silly photos of the four of us traversing the Vermont countryside, posing in front of scenic trash cans and grinning in fields of wild mustard which—in color—nearly match the complimentary T-shirts from the cycle-tour organizers whose logo is a holstein cow wearing sunglasses.

With this most recent tour, my "bicycle riding" had become cycling. There is a "cadence," I learned, which if maintained will make cycling nearly effortless. Ken and Simone from Hoboken, New Jersey, fellow cyclists on the tour, explained this to us at breakfast at the inn. Later, when our day's tour got underway, Ken and Simone, in their colorful spandex cycling shorts, followed us a mile or two out of town, and disappeared.

After that trip I got to thinking. The thing about our friends, Paul and Lois, is that they've stuck by us through cycling and a host of other things, too. We've mastered *this* cadence, if not the cycling cadence. This cycling tour was our third vacation together, not counting a few weekends in Columbus, Ohio, where we put in appearances at the health club attached to our hotel and the bakery in the French Market. Sometimes we travel with our children, sometimes not.

We have paid a heavy price for this friendship, for our life together is peppered with restaurant meals and lunches and coffee, bottomless glasses of iced tea, gallons of gasoline, a good number of picnics, and countless long-distance phone calls—an extravagant investment of love, time, and money.

Ours is a friendship forged through years of sharing life up close and personal. The babies we had in the same year are now in junior high. Our older two are in high school and college—they were one and three when we first met.

I remember one of those first evenings together. We sat in the living room of the rented mobile home where Paul and Lois lived—they didn't even have any of their own furniture yet. Jeremy fell asleep. It was the dead of winter and snowing, and Lois gave us a blanket to wrap him in for the short trip home.

They bought the house next door to ours, and I helped Lois move her clothes into her new closet. She had a lot of nice clothes back then and she still does. They have moved twice since, and we moved once. In every house they have shelves of books and more on the coffee table. So do we.

Late one night in the early years, we took a crazy notion to drive twenty miles to Poppin' Fresh Pies late at night—two kids in tow in their Dr. Dentons. The memory still serves us well as an inside joke—the restaurant went out of business years ago.

Back then we raided each others' cupboards—

didn't even ask to borrow a cup of sugar or a stick of mar-garine or a spool of thread—just helped ourselves. We don't pay back small debts or keep track of who left the tip last time. Lois likes coffee ice cream, and Paul doesn't drink coffee. We all listen to National Public Radio. Paul "pigs out" by eating a handful of M & M's. When the rest of us "pig out," we eat a whole bag of turtles or malted milk balls or Oreos.

When we were neighbors, Lois and I were highly domesticated. We baked oatmeal bread and tried vege-tarian recipes. We sewed clothes for ourselves and our children and hung wash on the line. We wallpapered to-gether and sat out on one or the other of our porch swings long after dusk, slapping mosquitoes and talking about life. Ralph and Paul both worked at Central Chris-tian High School, Ralph was attending night law school, and we didn't take vacations.

We planned our first vacation together the summer after Ralph took the bar exam. We went to Ocean City without our kids and rented cheap rooms about six blocks from the boardwalk. The house had the name

(Something) Arms. None of us can remember the name.

Lois and I dieted and exercised and got tan in preparation for the trip. We sewed ourselves outfits to wear on the boardwalk. We still agree that that summer we both looked better than we ever did before or since. The men don't remember how we looked.

Ralph, who had been studying for the bar exam all summer, was afraid he'd get a sunburn and used a sun block. Its uneven application resulted in a red-and-white spotted body. Afternoons he sat on the porch in one of the old wooden rockers reading pulp mysteries.

Our rooms each had a foot-wide aisle beside the bed. We shared the bathroom with Paul and Lois. There was a door (with a hook) in each bedroom, so it was possible to enter the tiny cubicle from either room. The walls were so thin we could almost hear each other breathing. One evening, after dinner on the boardwalk, we decided to go our separate ways. Ralph and I wanted to go to a movie but then decided not to. Somehow or other we ended up back in the Arms. Paul and Lois were in their room, but they didn't know we were in ours!

When I start listing these events, it is surprising how many things I remember about the fun we had together. We took our families with us and spent a week in Sarasota during the summer. Paul talked us into renting bikes and cycling along Longboat Key. One of the kids flopped her bike into a bush with leaves which stuck to her clothes. We bought her a new outfit in one of the pricey stores in St. Armands. I have a snapshot of the four of us that a waitress took while we were lunching in some elegant café. Our faces are beet red and our hair is damp.

• • •

I have only related the upswing of the cadence. There is another whole litany, describing the other side of our friendship. There is the night when the phone kept ringing next door on an evening they were away until we were sure something terrible had happened. It had. We shared their pain when we learned Lois's brother had drowned. We remember the trips to the hospital late at night when one of us was sick. The long, fearful vigil when nine-month-old Annie had a tumor. The scary accident when our whole family was hurt and they came. The career decisions, parenting difficulties, and other very personal things—which we shared in confidence and somehow saw each other through.

There are, of course, the petty annoyances we each sometimes feel when the others disappoint us. There have been misunderstandings, disagreements, and unkind words spoken. But those things never yet outweighed the wonderful memories of the fun we've had together. I am convinced that there is some mysterious blend of personalities that make the four of us so very complementary. Honest, transparent, and unpretentious when we're together, we are able simply to be ourselves. Our shared identity and history has revealed our weaknesses and flaws, and by some miracle we love each other anyway!

Our mutual memories and continuing vital friendship—these are things that keep us moving together in the same direction, up hills together, in the hot sun or in a downpour. This is the cadence of friendship.

*Marriage*

### TIED DOWN

I love the easy way
you pull on your clothes
to face each day
with equanimity.
You stand at the mirror
tying that knot
adjusting it—just so
around your neck.
From the bed I watch
and love your face.
I love you for
the man you are—
although I can't yet
understand part of your
complicated self.
Your knot draws pain
and pleasure in my heart.
How can you know?
You tie the knot each morning
tie it well. It seems
I know you less
from day to day
yet somehow ever
love you more and more.

# On Doing an Intimate Lunch

"WILL THIS BE SEPARATE CHECKS?" the waitress asks quizzically as she comes to take our order for lunch.

My partner and I exchange a confidential smile.

"No, we're together."

Our once- or twice-weekly lunch dates are a pleasant routine Ralph and I have established. Until now I'd never stopped to think how we must look: a "young middle-aged" twosome, dressed in typical business clothes, laughing and talking or engaged in spirited debate—and enjoying each other. What an odd couple, happily married. Couples who do *lunch* in restaurants aren't usually married. Married couples eat silent dinners together later in the day.

"My relationship with my husband is the best and most deeply satisfying experience of my life," I found myself saying to a friend who was about to marry.

"What a wonderful testimony!" she exclaimed.

Sometimes I think the joy and satisfaction of holy matrimony is one of the best-kept secrets of the Christian community. It's as if Christians were therapists: when they discuss marriage, they are teaching communication skills, solving problems, or trying to prevent divorce. Only recently did someone think to study the happily married couples. What such studies revealed provides a hopeful picture of the future of marriage. Why don't we talk about the good in our marriage relationships?

Marital health can be thought of as a continuum with indifference and divorce at one end and total marital well-being on the other. Most of us aren't at either end, but somewhere in the middle. Christians, like those in the secular world, often tend to focus on the wrong end of the line when they talk or write about marriage.

When I write about my satisfaction with marriage, I am not indulging in hyperbole. I believe it. I believe it in spite of the times things do not go well for us. We've had our share of conflict, frustration, and disappointment with each other and with our relationship. Our marriage isn't perfect, but when things go wrong, always in a day or two, we somehow manage to seek out one another again and do another lunch.

We still have some things to learn about handling conflict—we're working on it. But we always know within ourselves that the fights and "discussions," which have sometimes gone on into the night, will be put to rest in a day or two (we've let the sun go down a time or so upon our wrath; I'm not Gideon). We continue doing the hard work of keeping our relationship healthy, knowing that as long as we care enough to work at conflicts, they are not a threat to our solidarity.

It isn't easy to explain what a healthy, happy marriage is, but I think those of us who have one should try harder. It's important for those who have good marriages to talk about what makes their marriages good. We need to put words to the wedding music, explore what makes our relationships work, and believe in the best we discover about ourselves.

A good word is *intimacy.* Intimacy in marriage

doesn't mean you're always happy, always get what you want, solve all your problems before bedtime, or always feel romantic. But a couple who never discovers intimacy will never know deep marital satisfaction.

Clare Schumm, who worked in family-life ministry for a time, once described intimacy like this: "Intimacy requires mutual trust, the readiness to reach out beyond our own tiredness, hurts, and joys, to hear the other. Intimacy is best founded on shared tasks that lead to shared hearts and souls. It can sneak up on you and may often first be discovered in a tender moment."

Clare described seven aspects of intimacy, listed by psychologist David Olson. As I studied them, I realized that these key phrases may be one way to describe a satisfying marriage relationship. Different kinds of intimacy: physical, emotional, social, intellectual, recreational, and spiritual, all lead us in the direction of a satisfying marriage relationship.

Physical and sexual intimacy is an obvious place to start thinking about marital intimacy. In a study of happy marriages, one author found that more than any other quality of the relationship, it was the couple's faithfulness to the marriage vows which was taken for granted and commented on only briefly. Physical intimacy is the "of course" of the relationship. A quiet thing, expected.

In this department, I guess Ralph and I are an unusual couple in many ways by today's standards. I've thought about it sometimes recently, how unique we are, both monogamous—lifelong monogamy! No one I know ever brags about that. The media is full of discussions about "safe sex," and Dan Quayle dares to suggest abstinence to teens, but *no one* brags about being monoga-

mous. It's something I'm proud of, and I'm looking forward to many more years of blissful monogamy. Neither of us would dream of living our life any other way.

Emotional intimacy, enriching and nourishing sexual intimacy, is a special closeness couples share: the private jokes, the secret messages which pass between a couple without a word being spoken, the shared history, the layers of meaning in a family ritual. There were conversations between Ralph and me that took place long ago and yet remain so vivid that I could tell you our exact location and quote verbatim the words we said. Special moments of emotional intimacy shape our relationship and keep us going when something causes temporary distance between us.

Social intimacy is the enjoyment we've found in having mutual friends. The people we've spent time with over the years, whether we've gone out to dinner, been part of a small group, gone to the theater, or even embarked on a shared vacation with another family.

Intellectual intimacy has grown between us as we've grown up together. I don't think anyone thought of me as an intellectual when we were newlyweds. Lucky for me, I married a man who loves to read (he often reads a book a week), keeps up with world events, and knows how to start and keep a good conversation going. I'm a different person from the one I was when Ralph and I started out together. I'm more sure of myself and more free to express my opinions. My husband has encouraged that and accepted the "new me." These days I can almost hold my own in a friendly duel of ideas.

Ralph's first gift to me was a tennis racquet. Unfortunately, the promised lessons weren't too successful, but finally this past summer a new tennis racquet got me back into the swing of learning to play tennis. Recreational intimacy has been found as we share a goal of staying physically fit. Walking or cycling country roads together has provided us with some of our most intimate moments. (The other evening we were having an intense discussion on a late-night walk when another couple suddenly emerged in front of us. What did they hear?) We believe it's important, as a couple, to do things together, and we keep finding ways to spend recreational time working in our yard, going to the movies, or getting involved in community events.

Spiritual intimacy includes all of the everyday sharing we do as we talk about our values and how they affect our work, our children, our friendships, and our plans for the future. It includes talk about our joys and our successes and our deepest spiritual needs and struggles. It includes the prayers we offer for our children, ourselves, and others we care for. It stretches to include the new things we are learning about ourselves. Spiritual intimacy brings us to worship together and enables us to offer our individual lives and our mutual relationship to God.

If Ralph leads the way in recreational and intellectual intimacy, I think I forge ahead in the aesthetic intimacy department. On more than one occasion, I've turned from total absorption in light opera or a captivating drama to find my husband snoozing. But he is usually the one to light a fire in the fireplace on a winter evening. He will put aside the newspaper to read a story or listen to a poem I enjoyed. It is true that he walks too fast in antique stores or art museums, but together we admire the beauty of the changing seasons from our deck.

Oh yes, marriage has its difficult moments, even its difficult seasons. All levels of intimacy are not always present. Some marriages never manage to achieve all seven kinds of intimacy, but it's a goal worth pursuing. When things aren't going well, it might be good to take an inventory and shore up the weak areas by changing some habits.

According to one study, happy couples shared many activities and interests. Each individual in these successful marriages learned to look for ways to share life together. The conventional wisdom did not universally apply to them: "for breakfast, for dinner, but never for lunch."

Intimacy is built on togetherness. Why not do lunch with your spouse?

## MILKHOUSE TERROR

Black buckle boots
flapping at thick ankles
barn flavored overalls
damp, milky air.

The wet floor
is slippery
and the dusty old radio
playing on a shelf
in the corner
keeps time to the
clanking milk can lids.

Moist hot breath
and chlorine
etch shame
into a child's soul.

Swallowed milk tears
gag and choke
the memory of a boy
who never was
but might have been.

# Will Work for Food

IN *SECOND TREE FROM THE CORNER*, E. B. White has Trexler saying, "Forty years, and I still can't stay on life's little bucky horse." That pretty well sums up my feeling now and again when a black mood moves in and renders me temporarily incompetent.

Do I fit the pattern of writers who are mentally unbalanced? Wayne, of the film *Wayne's World*, would call me "mental." Or maybe all people are "mental," and only writers tell about it. My actions are absolutely appalling when I fall off the bucky horse. Some poverty of spirit indwells me, causing me to flounce around the house, slamming cupboard doors and throwing clothes in the washer, wielding the vacuum cleaner as if it were a weapon, pouting and acting the martyr.

The most awful snide and snotty comments pour forth from my mouth in response to absolutely anything anyone says to me. At 11:30 p.m. I'm dead on my feet but still ironing—the dedicated washerwoman! Crying, though unable to explain why, except to recognize that I'm a woman inside a body that makes me miserable.

Life must go on—incompetent or not—on to the food warehouse for my monthly stock-up buying, telling myself that my great joy in life, my great excitement for the day, is shopping at Food 4 Less, filling my cart with bargains, and cashing in coupons. There is a big yellow smiley face sign where I enter the store. It reads: "Smile, You're going to save money." It usually makes me laugh, but today it bugs me.

I park beside a beat-up, old sedan. There's a mother and a bunch of little kids in it. The windows are steamed up. I buy $79 worth of food, pack it into my mesh shopping "re-bags," haul it to the car, and load it into my trunk. When I come back from the cart return, I notice the same car, kids and mom still there. I've been in the store for a long time. The kids are moving around a lot.

Driving out of the plaza parking lot, I notice a trim attractive man with graying, wavy hair standing in the median strip between the lanes of traffic. He has on thick black gloves and a denim jacket. He is holding a small piece of corrugated cardboard, a sign which he directs toward me: WILL WORK FOR FOOD.

I avert my eyes and pretend to be watching the traffic. The light stays red too long. Long enough to think about the cartons of "light" yogurt, the family pack of steak, the 69-cent loaf of Italian bread, the cans of soup, the gallon of milk, and all the rest. Especially the unnecessary bottles of Diet Rite pop.

Most of the time, homeless families and hungry people have been invisible to me. Do they hide out in parking lots of grocery stores? When they become visible, I don't know what to do with them, especially when my trunk is full of groceries. I think about my sister-in-law, Carol, in Honduras, and I begin to understand her struggle. What do you do when beggars come to your door on a daily basis?

It angers me that people in North America are living in their cars and carrying signs begging for food and work. Mostly I am frustrated by my own predicament. For increasingly, it seems my family is rich, one of the richest, living among the poor. How long will it be until beggars start coming to *my* door?

What then? What desperation would drive an attractive middle-aged American to write a sign on corrugated cardboard and stand holding it in the middle of a busy intersection? Is he perhaps the father of the children in the car? Should I have given him my milk and steak? Stopped and talked? Directed him to some agency or church? Invited him home to do my yard work?

Is it enough to pray for him? No, perhaps not. But what to do? I do nothing. Later, a day or two, a week or two, there is a piece on the editorial page explaining the whole scene away. The sign-makers are manipulative and dishonest, the writer says, and we shouldn't be duped by their bid for our pity. I desperately want to believe the writer is right, but my heart tells me something else.

Jean Philippi of Wooster's People to People Ministries assures me that rural Wayne County, Ohio, does indeed have homeless people. She is the one who called them the "invisible" homeless. Abandoned by husband or boyfriend, young women with small children gradually wear out their welcome in the homes of friends and relatives. As a last resort, they come to People to People and are given lodging in a local motel until they can arrange for housing and other assistance.

Statistics show that one third of the homeless in our country are children. Ohio's poor are increasing every year. It is estimated that it will take at least $600 to resettle a homeless family in Cleveland if affordable housing is available. Getting a roof over their heads is only the beginning of the long road to survival and independence.

It is easier to explain away homelessness than it is to talk myself out of one of my black moods. A seductive stroll through a shopping mall, an hour or two browsing through *Victoria* magazine, a consultation with a landscape service—any of these will often be enough to lift a momentary bleak mood. Indulging in covetous materialism, even vicariously, is usually all it takes for me to put the homeless out again.

Most of the time I conveniently forget that in my quest to become a disciple, Jesus calls *me* to become homeless, if not in actuality, then in attitude. For the disciple, "stuff" shouldn't matter too much. That's hard to manage, living where I do.

Jesus told the wealthy young politician to sell all he had and give to the poor. I can handle the story if I don't take it too literally; after all, the Bethany siblings owned a nice home. The important thing is the attitude of generosity, caring and being *willing* to help.

My shallow Christianity embarrasses me as much as this inability to circumvent moods and pettiness. I need help, for I too am a beggar, at the mercy of a wealthy and generous God. I too stand at the intersection holding a flimsy cardboard sign, making a bid for some temporary solution.

And lo, Jesus stops and offers grace.

# *Technology*

## COMPU-PSALM

I will sing your praises,
   Oh, my IBM compatible!
      How excellent is your word.
You have set a screen at my right hand
   And a printer on my left.
Your user's manual is ever before me;
   Your tutorial and help key
      Are my salvation.
When I consider your keyboard
   And the work of my fingers,
      It is too wonderful for me.
Your overtype mode,
   Who can understand it?
You setteth your prompts in motion,
   You searchest my documents
      And sendeth them afar.
         Who can recover them?
Your menus and files are a mystery
   Who can know it?
Yea, your high-resolution monitor
   Is ever before me.
      In the watches of the night
      It is with me.
You paginateth my manuscript
   With headers and footers
      You justifieth my margins
         You restoreth my document.

You preparest a menu before me
In the presence of my errors.
My disk runneth over.
Surely insert and delete will be with me
All the days of my life
And I will dwell on a disk drive forever.

# Fax of Life

BESIDE A ROAD WE TRAVEL frequently, a little out-houselike structure suddenly appeared one day at a roadside intersection. It took only a second glance to realize what we were looking at. There snuggled up to a telephone pole was an Amish phone booth. The Amish phone-booth phenomenon seems irrational to many. But those who understand know that these rural roadside telephones, requested by Amish folk and sheltered in booths they built, are the Amish way of using technology without being owned by it.

The first thing one notices when visiting an Amish family is the calm, quiet simplicity of their homesteads. The creaking windmill and hay winch and the soft plodding of workhorses' hooves on sod remind me that my technology is noisy. Inside an Amish home on a midwinter afternoon, the dim light from a kerosene lamp prompts me to wonder what life would be like if one spent long, dark, quiet evenings without a television, radio, computer, or microwave oven. We envy them the quiet simplicity of their lives, but we can't imagine living without our conveniences.

Unlike the Amish, we begin our workday listening to recorded phone messages, living our lives against a backdrop of computer beeps, printer chatter, intercom buzzes, and roaring household appliances. Some of us

have built a lifework around the use, repair, or mainte-
nance of these powerful minimachines, which have in-
vaded our lives and now control our environment and
time. We add a fax number to our business letterhead.
We scramble to get more done in a shorter length of time
so we can do more. The more we accomplish, the more
we expect of ourselves. We no longer have the luxury of
pausing to wind a watch, or waiting for the rotary dial on
the telephone. Frequently called phone numbers are di-
aled at the touch of one button.

With the coming of the electronic age, a major
communication revolution has arrived, and most of us
are scurrying to get aboard. According to biblical story-
teller Thomas E. Boomershine, it took over a thousand
years for Israel to adapt to the writing medium and several hundred more for Christianity to appropriate it. He
says that our Scriptures were probably first chanted from
memory in a highly expressive manner and were inter-
preted in relation to new situations as they were told.
When manuscript was finally accepted, written stories
were read to the community, and oral interpretation was
given. Judaism continued in the oral tradition and adopted writing in strict subordination to the spoken word.

Was Ezra the first daring scribe who committed to
parchment all those dramatic stories and songs his con-
temporaries shared around their Hebrew dinner tables?
One can imagine the discussions that must have gone on
in the elders' meeting before they gave Ezra the "okay."

"Why do we need the stories written down, any-
way? I think the way we've been doing it is just fine. I say,
if you write down these stories of Abraham and Moses
and Joseph, people are going to quit telling stories alto-

gether. And once you get all of that written down, people will just go off in a corner by themselves and read instead of listening to each other—talking and asking questions and all of that."

"I don't think this writing thing is a good idea. How can you be sure that no error creeps into the text? People are going to get all hung up on what certain words mean and sit there picking it apart instead of applying the stories to their lives."

"What if the scribes get sloppy and don't proofread carefully?" another might have asked.

"Yes, and what about ethics? How will the next generation know they can believe what is written? What standards will you use to decide which stories to write?" questioned another.

"We trust *you* to write it, but what's to prevent others, less qualified, from using the pen?"

These fearsome dangers of the printed page have been eroded by the greater calamity of the electronic information age. Massive changes are occurring in the way we communicate. Encyclopedias are pulled from a "bookshelf" on the computer screen. Some predict the demise of books completely. Information is stored on compact discs or retrieved from data banks across the country via satellite or cable. Christians have jumped in wholeheartedly, loading the Scriptures into their computers and enhancing Bible study with the stroke of a word-search function key.

We, unlike the Hebrew teachers, have been quick to accept the gifts of technology. And we rarely question its advantages or consider the blight it might create in the way we relate to each other. We are convinced that technology has the ability to broaden our vision and widen our horizons, never stopping to question the way it separates us and distances us from each other—and even from our very inner selves.

Technology has enabled us to travel to distant countries. It has become routine—is seen as almost essential—for youth and young adults to experience other cultures. Churches send youth groups to Costa Rica, Venezuela, and Jamaica. College students regularly hop on a fast plane to China.

It may be that our travels will eventually turn us around, showing us the way to become what futurist Tom Sine calls "the countercultural presence of God." We travel to third world countries carrying our technology in a nylon duffel bag. But while we're there, we discover the beauty of handwoven straw baskets, the joy of three-hour afternoon siestas, the flavor of home-cooked stews. We marvel at the luxury of time for relationships. Life slows down, the chaff sifts off. Our spirits are energized by our observation and participation in the joyous worship celebrations of African Christians.

Coming home, we realize we are poorer than we first thought. We revise our notion of third-world people and "underdeveloped" nations. Some of us have even begun to shinny down off our technological pedestal and have begun to recognize that the two-thirds world has much to offer *us*. We understand better our need for face-to-face, hand-to-hand, heart-to-heart contact with others. We need to participate as well as to observe. To create as well as to operate. To recreate as well as to achieve.

Our toys must not blind us. Instead, we listen to

those who bring this new international version of global awareness. Our hope is in this vision of the simpler life we encounter elsewhere. Perhaps we should reexamine our wholesale acceptance of the trappings of a culture that places machines and materials in our hands but in exchange extracts living spirituality, human interaction, and the leisurely paced life. For it is these neglected and forgotten intangibles that give life meaning.

Taming technology sounds like a difficult task after one has luxuriated in the joy of writing on a computer and exulted in the freedom of microwaving lunch. But if we would become a truly countercultural presence of God, we must control our technology instead of letting it control us. We too must build a booth and place our technology by the side of the road.

## ORACLE

Beat down.
Beat down with fists.
Beat down with hammers.
Beat M-14s into
   tools for the farmer,
      wells for the desert,
         pumps for the irrigation ditch.

Walk in the furrow of peace.
Tread out destruction.
March to the cadence of truth.
Return to the farm.
Send soldiers to till the soil.

Beat down.
Beat down with fists.
Hammer out justice.
The river of Zion
   runs in the veins
      of the plowman.

# Jungle War and Desert Operation

SOUTHEAST ASIAN REFUGEES that I know, are no longer refugees. They are friends of my son, Jeremy. Phoumano Bannavong, who goes by "Paul," spent part of this afternoon helping Jeremy rig up his stereo equipment. Earlier today I proudly showed visiting relatives the prom portrait of Jeremy and Seo Luangraj. Seo spends a lot of time at our house now; I appreciate her infectious laughter and considerate manner.

One day I asked Seo about her departure from Laos. Like my other Southeast Asian friends, including some I helped to sponsor years ago, Seo's family suffered in ways we cannot fathom. "My parents expect a lot of me," Seo tells me. I understand: they have endured much to bring her to a life they believe to be worth living.

Seo, and others like her, are a societal reminder of the Vietnam War. Probably the most pleasant memory. Vietnam is a pain that doesn't go away. I tried to tell Seo what it was like to be a teenager in the United States during the Vietnam era. I told her that back then I tried to ignore the war; but it was impossible to disregard. It is a war that lingers still. The memories are an open wound, still festering in the psyche.

I recall the relentless obsession of the media back then to bring home the Vietnam War. Camera crews lived in the jungle and filmed the horror. We, the viewers, suffered with our soldiers but never completely hated the enemy. Everyone knew someone who was touched in some way by the war. My husband still has letters sent from Vietnam by a friend who came home in a box.

In my high school days, I used to flee the living room rather than have to see more body bags and coffins draped with American flags coming home. The black and white television we watched back then did little to dim the horror of this dirty war that we hated with a passion. The thatch-roofed huts in Southeast Asian jungles were real to me. People lived in those houses and tended their rice paddies. I never grew accustomed to the recorded thump of military helicopters; it was horrible, even in the absence of Dolby sound.

And at the end of every newscast, when they gave the body count, I knew what this war was costing my nation. What it was costing me. Vietnam was a war with a human dimension, a human cost. When I look at Seo, I remember that war forever changed the life of a little girl and her family who escaped to us across the Mekong River.

●　●　●

This week, author Kurt Vonnegut came to Canton. I went to Kent State University's Stark Campus to hear him speak about war and about writing. "I hear Stormin' Norman Schwarzkopf was in the neighborhood this week," he quipped. He was referring to the general's appearance the night before at Cleveland's Front Row Theater.

After commenting on Schwarzkopf's camouflage uniform (which he satirically described as looking like a

Spanish omelette), Vonnegut opined that this war showed us to be "utterly without pity." Operation Desert Storm stands in contrast to other wars, Vonnegut told his audience of writers and would-be writers: earlier leaders expressed deep sorrow for the victims of war and even for the enemy. "You could see the pain on the faces of Eisenhower and MacArthur. Lincoln recognized the bravery of the Confederate soldiers in his Gettysburg Address. But now, we are utterly without pity."

I returned home and read again last night's newspaper account of General Schwarzkopf's speech. It was just as Vonnegut had said: " 'When we were done, Saddam had the *second* largest army in Iraq,' Schwarzkopf joked, referring to Saddam's claim of having the fourth largest army. 'I don't need to tell you who had the first. . . .' " And on it went. Operation Desert Storm, if you listen to Norman, was a clean, beautiful war.

In contrast, the Vietnam War gave us nothing to brag about and sent us no effervescent general to make us feel good. Yet historians now believe it was, in part, the media coverage that brought an end to the Vietnam War. There is a limit to our tolerance when we are forced to view the human cost of a war night after night in our living rooms.

But *this* time, in *this* war, our cameras were muzzled, and it was all over in a matter of weeks. It didn't take years like in Vietnam. Someone, this time, knew enough to keep us from being horrified at the cost of war. This time we were protected, and educated, and properly informed. At the beginning of this war, our president came on national television and urged us to be "champions of freedom." Yet only a few days before, the Pentagon had given news reporters strict guidelines about how news of the war could be reported: no live television pictures from the front, newspeople are to be accompanied at all times by military personnel, there will be security reviews of all reports, and no graphic pictures of dead or wounded soldiers will be allowed.

Some of us were finally grateful that the media had the good sense to refer to the war, named "Operation Desert Storm" by public relations specialists, as the "Gulf War." Still, Gulf War logo and the newscasters' Parker Brothers' Middle East board game (complete with movable plastic game pieces) gave war all the panache of a television miniseries or a sports event.

*Newsweek* recently quoted the words of a Pentagon official on why U.S. military censors refused to release video footage of Iraqi soldiers being sliced in half by helicopter cannon fire: "If we let people see that kind of thing, there would never again be any war." Indeed!

Descriptive and deceptive phrases were employed to combat our need to know. "Operation Desert Storm" was rarely called a "war" by our military personnel. Our missiles made "surgical strikes." Our allied forces joined in an "air campaign." We flew "missions" and "sorties" to "neutralize" our "targets" with "tactical strikes." Our Tomahawks, Wild Weasels, and Stealth Fighters "pounded" Iraq, while our noble Patriot missiles fended off Scuds—a weapon with a vulgar-sounding name that could only belong to the enemy.

"Our nation," declared President Bush, "is the only nation to assemble the *forces of peace*." We failed to gag when we were fed the line about "peace-keeping forces."

The Gulf War sought to engulf us in technology and rhetoric, and we acquiesced. At one time our government needed our bodies to wage a war; now they need only our dollars and our approval. They commandeer our assent to the carnage by preventing us from experiencing, even vicariously, the human cost of war. They entertain us with the jovial four-star General Schwarzkopf, whose name symbolizes himself. Erich Fromm's words now seem prophetic: "We have built machines which act like men and developed men who act like machines."

Images of this recent war were made to seem almost beautiful: a colorful collage of yellow and orange ribbons which patriotic Americans had tied around fence posts and plastered on front doors; red, white, and blue flags; glittering missiles that lit up the desert sky; and a jolly decorated general who joked about our destruction of the enemy.

Kurt Vonnegut says we are "utterly without pity." God must agree with him.

About writing: Vonnegut claims that the foremost quality needed to become a good writer is passion. I wonder if there is anything a passionate writer (or a corps of them) could possibly do to prevent another war.

## PSALM OF MOSES

Your voice is a fire, Lord.
Earth shoes prohibit
Holy Presence.

Ease pain of royal losses
faded glory
failed duty
the lost era.

Chart me a way through
recalcitrant king
unyielding sea
searing desert.

Pursuing armies drown in terror
swallowed in by power
and civic pride.

Dwellers in
trust-building wilderness.
Drink melting manna—
foaming water
from solid rock.
Shekinah Glory
sweep Egyptian skies!

Count not Egyptian losses.
Weep not for all
relinquished treasure.
Lean upon the rod.

Clutch in silence
the sturdy promise
of a Mighty God.
Trust this for passage
of uneven ground.

Tread on in silence
toward a distant Sinai
and fashion in thy heart
some new Jerusalem.

# Vacation with Disaster

THIS TIME WHEN WE SAID our vacation was a disaster, it wasn't a joke. In the spring of 1990, the six families in our small group packed up cars and vans the week before Easter and headed for Moncks Corner, South Carolina. In this city Mennonite Disaster Service (MDS) had maintained a headquarters ever since Hurricane Hugo struck the Low Country on September 21-22, 1989.

Our entire work crew numbered twenty-nine and included six friends not part of our small group. Our children ranged in age from six through sixteen. Most of us arrived on Palm Sunday evening. Our son, Jeremy, had served with MDS earlier during a school miniterm, and our welcome proved to be just what he had predicted: "You'll walk in, and some guy at the desk who is a total stranger will greet you like he knows you—even though he doesn't."

It may be that MDS coordinator Wilbur Lentz from Middlebury, Indiana, didn't know us personally, but he already knew a lot about us the moment we walked through the door of the warehouse/dorm. Our Hugo Hilton was a former Pepsi bottling company, located across the road from Burger King and not far from Walmart. Wilbur knew that we, like most other MDS volunteers, came with an assortment of skills, expectations, and interests, and that we were Mennonites looking for a way to help.

He realized that during our short stay he would barely learn to know us.

Wilbur knew that the carpenters in our group wanted to build a house, and that most of the women wanted to climb up on a roof and catch some sun while pounding nails. From experience, he knew it would be hard to find kitchen help willing to get up and flip pancakes and pack lunches at 5:00 a.m. and that few people really enjoy sanding drywall in small homes occupied by people with their belongings stashed around the room in plastic garbage bags to protect them from the leaking roof. Wilbur could only hope some of us might come back to serve a second or third week before MDS closed up the files and headed for home or to some future disaster months from now.

That day we stepped into Wilbur's office, most of us had never encountered disaster close up. It had been months since the hurricane hit, but reminders were still everywhere. Hugo chewed up 90 percent of all the trees in Berkeley County, snapping off tall pines eight to ten feet from the ground as if they were toothpicks. Giant trees fell across houses, flying debris crashed into windows, and whole roofs, porches, mobile homes, and houses were twisted out of shape and moved. Some wreckage came to rest in a garden or the next-door neighbor's backyard or simply disappeared entirely. Friendly shade trees, lifelong companions to houses and their occupants, crashed into those houses, leaving residents exposed to the elements.

What could we do in the face of so much disaster?

Our crew moved into the two dorm rooms. The women got the ward carpeted in "Charleston" green. It was lined with Salvation Army cots on each long wall. (By the end of the week, those dorm rooms had earned the Mennonite Disaster label in their own right!)

We could reach the makeshift shower by walking a short piece through the warehouse stacked with donated building supplies of every description, not all of them useful. When our larger-than-normal group of women arrived, an MDS leader solved the shower scarcity by crayoning "Ladies" on the back of the "Men's" sign. Now the room could do double duty with the flip of a cardboard sign. Above all else, everyone was warned, "Do not play practical jokes with the shower door sign!"

On that first night, and every night of our stay afterward, we gathered in the big dining room and ate good Mennonite cooking—mashed potatoes, Swiss steak, green beans with ham floating in butter. We sat on assorted worn and dented folding metal chairs at tables fashioned from doors. A television and a VCR were flanked by a table of magazines for evening browsing—for those lucky enough to get the overstuffed sofa and chair. The dog-eared *Vogue* and *Glamour* somehow seemed strangely out of place. No need for eye makeup here. A basketball hoop in the back of the warehouse provided evening recreation for anyone who still had energy to spare at day's end.

Stan Kamp, a carpenter in our group, was on his second trip to South Carolina; for MDS. He helped project assistant Dan Bontrager make assignments for our group members. Each evening Stan and Dan got their heads together and decided our fate for the next day. The youngest children were directed by two or three adults from our group and were sent to outdoor cleanup or painting jobs. One day they worked in the warehouse and grounds, helped bake cookies, and washed dishes. Unskilled adults in our group were sent out in teams with other short-term volunteers, headed by the more skilled workers. The odds favored most of us working on roof or ceiling repair. A top priority for MDS was providing help for the uninsured. Seven months after Hugo, low-income families were struggling to repair roof damage.

Each morning we arose early, got into our "grubbies," and took off in one of the five MDS vans, which had been loaded with basic tools and supplies. Many of the building supplies were taken from the stacks of donated materials in the warehouse. Into the van also went a water jug and our coolers, filled with the regulation MDS lunch.

On our first day, four of us worked for Esther Williams and Eliza Judge, elderly black women who lived in Pineville. Pineville could hardly be called a village. It was a cluster of tiny, cottage-type homes far from any urban area. When I saw it, there were few pines left in the settlement. This was the Low Country the tourist books write about, but I suspect few tourists will ever experience the setting as we did.

The carpenters unloaded their tools, ready to finish a back porch. Wilbur, our leader that morning, explained to us that although MDS policy is to restore living space, not make other home improvements, the porch was Mrs. William's laundry area. We entered the small kitchen through the back door, carrying a bucket of drywall compound, tools, and a large roll of plastic. Our job, Wilbur explained, was to finish ceilings in a bedroom, dining room, and living room, and to finish patching two bedroom ceilings. On the previous day, other volunteers had hung sheet rock in the crooked little house that seemed to be stuffed with belongings, including several pieces of new upholstered furniture and new carpets.

We spread sheets of the omnipresent plastic across the bed and pushed the end behind stacks of clothes piled in the corner. It was good to discover that most of us could reach the low ceilings without a ladder. Mrs. Williams, wearing a white knit stocking hat fastened with a safety pin, walked through the room and tuned her portable radio to an African-American gospel station. We started slinging mud as if we knew what we were doing. Most of us had never done more than fill a nail hole when painting a bedroom; now here we were finishing new drywall! In the face of disaster, it didn't matter.

Esther Williams was grateful, excessively so. She told us we were sent from God and that her prayers had been answered when MDS came. We were angels of mercy, she insisted. "I'm just so thankful. The Lord is so good! I'll be prayin' for y'all."

Esther told us how she had cooked out in her yard for days after the storm. It was seven weeks until her electricity was finally restored. We listened as she mourned the loss of her large pecan tree, her pines, and the china-berry bushes.

We stopped our work to hear her lament because we'd been told earlier that part of our mission was to be there to listen; many of these people were suffering from stress or depression as a result of the storm. Now they were beginning to have a more normal life, but their losses remained open wounds. Many told of sitting through the six- to seven-hour storm, not sure whether they would live or die. They were in shock and didn't think to apply for help or didn't know how to go about it. Many of these homes were in poor condition to begin with. Often it was difficult to separate hurricane damage from earlier neglect. Most homeowners MDS helped were needy and had no insurance. "We're here to help the people," Wilbur told me. "You go the second mile, probably the third."

MDS was working alongside a local interfaith committee that helped screen and select applicants for disaster aid. Altogether MDS had fourteen satellite stations of MDS workers in South Carolina; most of them bunked and had their meals in small community churches. MDS stayed in South Carolina for well over one year, long after most other aid agencies had left.

After eating our lunch of bologna sandwiches on white bread, and potato chips, Ralph and I hiked over to Eliza Judge's house. From the outside it appeared to be a neat cabin surrounded by an immense freshly plowed truck patch. Eliza, her thin graying hair braided into two wiry coils, greeted us from the porch where she sat shelling corn. Like most of her neighbors, she was burning debris in her yard and arose from her broken stool periodically to stir the fire. When I return to Pineville in my mind, I think of Eliza Judge standing there months after Hugo, head bowed over a rusted chipped hoe, contemplating slowly smoking pine embers.

Eliza's home—a cabin really—was more sparsely furnished and more crooked than the first house we'd worked in. We filled the holes and sanded ceilings in a tiny kitchen, dining room, and bathroom. Our arms and shoulders were beginning to ache, and our hair was covered with drywall dust. Ralph crawled through the tiny trap door to the attic, found the wire to Mrs. Judge's dining room light, and brought it through the ceiling. Our MDS predecessors had accidentally drywalled over it. I might add that we weren't particularly impressed with their work, yet we couldn't have done as well.

I noted the small testimonies of faith on Mrs. Judge's humble walls: a framed copy of "Footprints in the Sand," a "Bless and protect this house" motto.

Each day we were in Moncks Corner, we were given a different assignment and had a different experience. Ralph and I took our turn with the children and went on a long trek to the home of a recluse whose house was filled with cats and dogs. The children carried branches and stacked brush.

Several scenes startled us. Our daughter, Laura, told us she found a dead dog while doing cleanup at Vyola Beasley's house. Marion Beyeler, helping the children that day, removed it but "about lost his cookies." Jessica ate a box of Raisinets a grateful homeowner had given her, only to discover maggots in the last piece of candy. Sherri was kneeling on a mat of some sort while painting and suddenly realized it was a leathery dead animal.

The teenage boys actually tore down an entire house in one day in a village named Huger. One woman couldn't believe that children would give up their spring break to help hurricane victims. Parents had no trouble believing that those boys could tear down a house in a day!

Ralph and I finally had our turn on a roof, tearing off shingles and throwing them down, carting them off past several skinny barking dogs, securely chained to their doghouses. The rest room that day was behind the bushes near the place we dumped the threadbare shingles. Watch out for poison oak!

Another day we helped with some finishing chores in one of the new houses volunteers had built. Wilbur said that female MDS volunteers enjoyed trying new things, and he found plenty of things for them—and us— to do: installing light fixtures and doorknobs, finishing drywall, and painting.

The stock summation of many who return from a service trip is this: I received more than I gave; I learned more than I helped. Now I too experienced that truth and found myself toeing the party line. We reported that our MDS excursion was the best vacation our family ever had. Helping others created an inexplicable bond between us.

We all labored hard that week, but we also began to relax and unwind. We tempered our work ethic. "Slow down!" someone told us. "You're in the South." At day's end we laughed and told stories and shared our experiences with the rest of the group. We began to look at our own lives with new perspective. We arrived with apprehension about our carpentry skills, wondering what we could contribute. We left knowing that our presence in the bayou country brought a measure of hope and courage to those we served.

# *Epilogue*

ANTIQUE SHOPS SHOWCASE treasures for my mother and me. We wander aimlessly through the several stores which have overtaken downtown Columbiana. This is pure recreation; we have no intention of buying. It is enough to look and trace memories: "Grandma Horst had an oak secretary desk something like that one," I say, seeing it clearly in my mind's eye as it stood so many years ago in the corner of her kitchen.

The reminders of Grandma Martin are even greater in these stores since she had a greater love of small things, trinkets: a pair of crystal drop lamps, a ceramic cookie jar in the shape of a gigantic apple, a gossip bench for the telephone. (Grandma didn't fit into the chair and kept it stacked full of old phone books.)

In at least one way, I am like my Grandma Martin, who kept voluminous scrapbooks, newspaper clippings of all the friends and relatives in her own expression of the Victorian era commonplace book. Yet my mother needs an explanation for why I keep a journal. She wonders if I'm not worried that someone might someday find my journals and read them. But I am fearless. Yes, my children and future grandchildren, and others too, may read them someday. If they do, I trust them to sift my words with love.

Perhaps in my writings they, like you, will glean traces of treasure from my quest for God in life's commonplace events. Here others may read the unanswered questions of my life—and the answers as they came, the pain and the triumph.

In difficult times I lean on the words of the poet Rainer Maria Rilke, who counsels me to "live the questions now. Perhaps you will then gradually, without noticing it, live along some distant day into the answer." I think those words provide a good philosophy. They speak of patience, of becoming a seeker, of looking to God for comfort, guidance, and peace.

Living the questions means I don't think long linear thoughts about outcomes. For the poet, the powerful poetic images of Isaiah are nearly enough to build a life on: beating swords into plowshares, preaching good news, proclaiming freedom to the captives—and always in the background, the illuminating image of Zion, the New Jerusalem.

Perhaps in our time poets are the prophets. We see the world in new ways and help others glimpse that vision. We are the proclaimers, the mystics, live-ers of the questions. The courage to pick up the pen comes from my personal belief that words *can* make a difference. They can heal, cause slight shifts in someone's thinking, and begin a communal experience of mutating metaphors in which someone else may build something new out of my words. I hope that my narrative will somehow contribute to God's kingdom as we live the questions in a community of compassion and hope, of spiritual disciplines and prayer, and of shouldering social responsibility.

Questions will always remain, for Christianity's outcomes are just the opposite of what you'd think: the captives are freed; the blind see; the kingdom belongs to the poor; the King is crucified; the dead rise from the grave. And the prophet has little to do with the outcome.

Life is partially mystery, and sometimes in our quest for God, we find each other and community. Perhaps we are, after all, at our spiritual best as we trace the pathway of life, treasure the commonplace, and along the way live out the questions of our time.

# *Author*

JOANNE LEHMAN IS AN EDITOR, journalist, and student of communication arts. After graduating from Central Christian High School (Kidron, Ohio) in 1968, Joanne attended Hesston (Kansas) College for one year.

Following marriage, Joanne and her husband, Ralph, entered Teachers Abroad Program (TAP) with Mennonite Central Committee in Marystown, Newfoundland. There she taught third grade for two years. Since then, she has taught Sunday school, Bible school, and workshops at Wayne Center for the Arts (Wooster, Ohio).

An enthusiastic homemaker, Lehman spent the first decade of her adult life as a seamstress, organizing and teaching sewing classes in fabric stores. In 1980, she answered a call to the ministry of writing. She had kept journals from the age of twelve, but now began to view writing as her vocation.

Lehman in 1987-93 served as the first woman and the first layperson to edit *Ohio Evangel,* a periodical of the Ohio Conference of the Mennonite Church. Her duties included desktop publishing and public relations along with reporting and writing. Joanne's editorials have been read widely in the conference circle and beyond. Her feature articles, poetry, and news reports have also been published in more than a dozen periodicals.

Early in 1994, Lehman began work as a community relations specialist, involved in community-based mental health education and promotion in Wayne and Holmes counties of Ohio.

In 1986 Lehman returned to college as a part-time student and is completing a bachelor's degree in communication arts/journalism at Malone College (Canton, Ohio). She was first runner-up for the 1991 National Federation of Press Women Junior-Senior Scholarship. Twice she has been awarded the Malone College Clarence J. Swallen Endowed Scholarship for students preparing for mission work or service in the church.

Lehman finds fulfillment in her life through nurturing her relationships, satisfying her curiosity, and indulging her creative impulses. Hobbies and interests include sewing and crafts, family recreation, and theater.

The author's husband, Ralph Lehman, is a partner in the law firm of Logee, Hostetler, Stutzman & Lehman. Their son, Jeremy (born 1974), is a college student married to Seo Luangraj. Their daughter, Laura (1981), is a middle-school student.

Joanne Lehman was born in Salem, Ohio, the daughter of Melvin and Pauline Horst of Columbiana, Ohio. While growing up she attended Leetonia Mennonite Church and now is a member of the Kidron (Ohio) Mennonite congregation.